Asperger Syndrome

This fully revised new edition is a clear and concise guide to effective classroom practice for teachers and assistants supporting children with Asperger syndrome. Written for use in mainstream schools and other non-specialist settings, the book provides accessible information on the latest developments in this area.

With examples of innovative strategies and approaches to facilitate progress in learning, this new edition:

- outlines the underlying impairments and their educational implications;
- explores the process of assessment and diagnosis in Asperger syndrome;
- offers practical strategies for effective and realistic classroom intervention, including access to the National Curriculum;
- considers the behavioural challenges the child with Asperger syndrome may pose;
- shows how transitions can be supported.

Asperger Syndrome: A Practical Guide for Teachers informs professionals meeting a child with Asperger syndrome for the first time and equips them with effective educational and behavioural intervention strategies. This new edition is also updated with reference to Every Child Matters, the Disability Equality Duty and Access Inclusion Planning.

This book is essential reading for professionals in mainstream schools, educational psychologists and INSET providers (including initial teacher training), as well as for parents and carers.

Val Cumine is a Regional Autism Tutor for Birmingham University, County Senior Educational Psychologist for Autism in Lancashire and an independent consultant and trainer specialising in autism.

Julia Dunlop is an early years and autism specialist, and is currently Senior Educational Psychologist for Blackpool local authority. She serves as a member of the Steering Group of the Autism Education Trust.

Gill Stevenson is a behaviour and autism specialist. She is currently Service Manager of the Service for Children with Complex Needs for Blackburn-with-Darwen local authority.

Asperger Syndrome

A practical guide for teachers

Second edition

Val Cumine, Julia Dunlop and Gill Stevenson

With illustrations by Sally Leach

Routledge
Taylor & Francis Group

LONDON AND NEW YORK

First edition published 1998 by David Fulton Publishers
Reprinted 1998 (twice), 1999 (three times), 2000 (three times), 2001, 2002, 2003, 2004, 2005

This edition published 2010
by Routledge
2 Park Square, Milton Park, Abingdon, Oxon OX14 4RN

Simultaneously published in the USA and Canada
by Routledge
270 Madison Avenue, New York, NY 10016

Routledge is an imprint of the Taylor & Francis Group, an informa business

Typeset in Garamond by
Keystroke, Tettenhall, Wolverhampton
Printed and bound in Great Britain by
MPG Books Group

British Library Cataloguing in Publication Data
A catalogue record for this book is available from the British Library

Library of Congress Cataloging in Publication Data
Asperger syndrome : a practical guide for teachers / Val Cumine, Julia Dunlop and Gill Stevenson.
   — 2nd ed.
      p. cm.
Includes bibliographical references and index.
1. Autism in children. 2. Autistic children—Education. I. Dunlop, Julia. II. Stevenson, Gill.
III. Title.
RJ506.A9C84 2010
618.92'858832—dc22   2009017574

ISBN 10: 0–415–48371–9 (pbk)
ISBN 10: 0–203–86486–7 (ebk)

ISBN 13: 978–0–415–48371–1 (pbk)
ISBN 13: 978–0–203–86486–9 (ebk)

Contents

Contents

Figures

About the authors

Val Cumine first encountered autism when completing her Masters at Nottingham Child Development Research Unit in the 1970s. She has retained an enduring interest since. Having worked as an educational psychologist and senior pre-school specialist, Val led the county-wide Autism Research Project for Lancashire in the 1990s. She is currently the county's Senior Specialist EP for Autism Spectrum Disorders, contributing to multi-agency assessment and intervention for early years and school-age children. Val is also a Regional Tutor for the Birmingham University Autism Distance Learning M.Ed and offers independent training and consultancy. Advances made in our understanding together with wonderfully innovative teaching and support strategies for children and young people on the autism spectrum have provided some of the most exciting and rewarding aspects of Val's career. It is a pleasure to once again promote awareness of these in the new edition of this practical guide to Asperger syndrome.

Julia Dunlop (formerly Leach) was, for 20 years, a teacher working in both special and mainstream schools. For eight years, she worked as part of a multi-agency assessment team in a child development centre. She first linked up with Val Cumine and Gill Stevenson in 1992 when they formed Lancashire's Autism Research Team. Qualifying as an educational psychologist in 1997, Julia is currently Senior EP in Blackpool, where she specialises in both early years and autism. She is delighted to be collaborating once again with Val and Gill in revising and updating their best-selling books.

Gill Stevenson taught in mainstream and special schools before becoming an advisory teacher for children on the autism spectrum. She currently manages an integrated team within Blackburn-with-Darwen Children's Services, who work with children and young people aged 0–19 who have complex needs and their families. The fascination with autism which began with the establishment of Lancashire's Autism Research Team has endured in the continuing working relationship with Val and Julia.

Preface

The first edition of this book stemmed from the authors' involvement in a three-year project, researching autism and Asperger syndrome in Lancashire. During that time, the authors met over 100 children with Asperger syndrome, in a variety of settings.

The content of this second edition draws on this previous and subsequent experience of working with children with Asperger syndrome in three local authorities in the north west of England.

The anecdotes in the book are all based on real children, but names have been changed for reasons of confidentiality.

The authors have met many parents of children with Asperger syndrome, but one deserves a special mention: Lynda Bannister, mother of John, who has written so eloquently and positively of her son's strengths and difficulties. We are pleased to again have the opportunity to quote directly from her writings. Lynda stands as a representative of all the parents and children from whom we have learnt so much.

Figure 0.1 Sebastian loves to follow the lines on the playground making the sound of a steam engine

CHAPTER 1

Asperger syndrome
An introduction

Who was Asperger?

Hans Asperger (1906–1980) lived and worked in Vienna. He qualified as a doctor and specialised in paediatrics. His work brought him into contact with a number of boys who found it difficult to 'fit in' socially. In addition to their poor social interaction skills, the boys had difficulties with the social use of language, together with a limited ability to use and understand gesture and facial expression. Also evident were repetitive, stereotypical behaviours, often with 'abnormal fixations' on certain objects.

Having noted the similarities in the behaviour of a number of these boys, Asperger (1944) wrote and presented his paper 'Autistic psychopathies in childhood'. He recognised how severely the boys' difficulties affected their everyday lives, commenting, 'they made their parents' lives miserable and drove their teachers to despair'. He was also aware of the boys' many positive features – they often had a high level of independent thinking, together with a capacity for special achievements – but he didn't underestimate the impact of their individuality on others with whom they came into contact, and he noted their vulnerability to teasing and bullying.

Asperger's paper was written in German towards the end of World War II, and for this reason reached only a limited readership. It only became widely accessible in the early 1980s when it was first translated into English and referred to by Lorna Wing in her own research into autism and related conditions. It was felt that the term 'Autistic psychopathy' sounded too negative, and 'Asperger syndrome' was suggested as a more acceptable alternative.

Autism and Asperger syndrome

At the same time as Asperger was doing his research in Vienna, the child psychiatrist Leo Kanner was working in Boston, USA. He saw a similar cluster of behaviours in a number of children whom he went on to describe as 'autistic' – using the same descriptor which Asperger had used for his research group. Both Kanner and Asperger had referred to the work of Bleuler (1911) when choosing the word 'autism'. However, Bleuler had used the term to describe people who had withdrawn from participation in the social world. Kanner stressed that the children he was describing had never been participants in that social world, whilst Asperger felt that the coining of the word 'autism' was 'one of the great linguistic and conceptual creations in medical nomenclature'.

For Kanner, 'early childhood autism', on which he wrote his (1943) paper 'Autistic disturbance of affective contact', had a number of defining features, including:

- a profound autistic withdrawal;
- an obsessive desire for the preservation of sameness;
- a good rote memory;
- an intelligent and pensive expression;
- mutism, or language without real communicative intent;
- over-sensitivity to stimuli;
- a skilful relationship to objects.

Later researchers, particularly Lorna Wing (1981b and 1991), compared Asperger's writings to Kanner's early papers and noted significant similarities between the children being described. The key difference was that the children described by Asperger had developed grammatical speech in infancy – although the speech they had was not used for the purpose of interpersonal communication.

The core difficulties in autism and Asperger syndrome are shared. Asperger syndrome involves a more subtle presentation of difficulties. This is not to say that it is a mild form of autism – as one parent said, 'My child has mild nothing'. Asperger syndrome affects every aspect of a child's life and can cause great upset for the family.

A commonly held view is that Asperger syndrome should be regarded as a sub-category of autism – part of the wider spectrum, but with sufficient distinct features to warrant a separate label. This view is useful for educational purposes as it is generally accepted that intervention and treatment approaches for children anywhere within the autism spectrum will share the same foundation.

The term 'Asperger syndrome' is useful in explaining to parents and teachers the root of the many problems they encounter with a child who is intellectually able, yet experiences significant social difficulties.

The triad of impairments in autism

While Asperger's paper lay undiscovered, Kanner's observations on the nature of autism were the subject of much discussion, debate and further research. Lorna Wing and Judith Gould (1979) carried out an extensive epidemiological study in the London borough of Camberwell. They concluded that the difficulties characteristic of autism could be described as a 'Triad of Impairments'.

They emphasised the fundamentally social nature of the three linked areas of difficulty:

- impairment of social interaction;
- impairment of social communication;
- impairment of social imagination, flexible thinking and imaginative play.

Wing and Gould noted that there were many children who did not exactly fit Kanner's description of 'early childhood autism', but who, nevertheless, had significant difficulties within the areas of the triad. This led Wing (1981a) to use the term 'Autistic continuum' and later (Wing 1996) 'the Autistic spectrum', allowing for a broader definition of autism based on the triad.

Many individuals with Asperger syndrome experience sensory processing difficulties which impact on their learning, behaviour and everyday functioning. It is not clear that sensory processing problems are central to the condition; however, it is considered that sensory issues can give rise to difficulties and need to be taken into account.

Diagnostic criteria

There is acceptance that autism is characterised by the co-occurrence of impairments in social interaction, social communication and social imagination, and diagnostic criteria are agreed on the basis of the triad.

In 1981, as a result of examining Asperger's original paper, Lorna Wing (1981a) outlined the following criteria for Asperger syndrome:

- impairment of two-way social interaction and general social ineptitude;
- speech which is odd and pedantic and stereotyped in content, but which is not delayed;
- limited non-verbal communication skills – little facial expression or gesture;
- resistance to change and enjoyment of repetitive activities;
- circumscribed special interests and good rote memory;
- poor motor coordination, with odd gait and posture and some motor stereotypes.

Whereas Asperger maintained that speech was acquired at the normal age, Wing disagreed. From her own experience, she found that half the population she would describe as having Asperger syndrome had not developed language at the normal age. Criteria developed by Christopher Gillberg (1989) were broadly similar.

Two major diagnostic instruments are currently in use by clinicians – the *Diagnostic and Statistical Manual*, 4th edition (*DSM IV*, American Psychiatric Association 1994) and the *International Classification of Diseases*, 10th edition (*ICD 10*, World Health Organisation 1992) (see Appendix). Both systems base their diagnostic criteria for Asperger syndrome on the three fundamental impairments outlined within the triad. Following Asperger, they rule out early language delay, and neither includes motor coordination difficulties as a diagnostic feature.

Numbers of children with Asperger syndrome

In 1993, Stefan Ehlers and Christopher Gillberg published the results of research which attempted to establish the prevalence of Asperger syndrome. It had been carried out in Gothenburg and involved studying children in mainstream schools. From the numbers they identified as having Asperger syndrome, they calculated a prevalence rate of 36 per 10,000, having used criteria which allowed for the presence of some early language delay.

Current estimates of prevalence, focusing on the whole spectrum of autistic conditions, suggest a best estimate of 1 in 100 children (Baird *et al.* 2006).

All prevalence studies have indicated that boys are far more likely to be affected than girls. Asperger himself had felt that it could be an exclusively male difficulty. Gillberg (1991) suggests that the ratio of boys to girls is in the region of 10:1.

Causes

As yet, the cause of Asperger syndrome is unknown. It is unlikely that there is a single cause – rather a set of triggers, any one of which, occurring at a certain time within a chain of circumstances, can cause Asperger syndrome.

Asperger thought that the condition was probably transmitted genetically, describing it as an 'inherited personality disorder'. Although current thinking is that Asperger syndrome is not directly inherited, continuing research looks at the possibility of some genetic basis.

Today, researchers are trying to pinpoint the areas of the brain which function differently in Asperger syndrome. As technology improves, affected areas are being more precisely indicated.

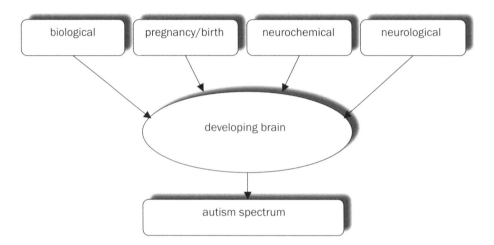

Figure 1.1 Factors which may trigger conditions on the autism spectrum

Summary

- Asperger syndrome is a condition which is thought to fall within the spectrum of autism – with enough distinct features to warrant its own label.

- It was first described in 1944 by Austrian Hans Asperger, whose work was first published in English in 1991.

- It is characterised by subtle impairments in three areas of development: social communication, social interaction and social imagination. There are, in some cases, additional motor coordination and organisational problems.

- It affects people in the average to above-average ability range.

- The overall prevalence of children and young people on the autistic spectrum is estimated to be 1 in 100.

- Boys are more likely to be affected than girls, with a suggested ratio of 10 boys to every girl.

Assessment and diagnosis

Key features of Asperger syndrome

Asperger syndrome is characterised by subtle impairments in three areas of development. There are, in some cases, additional motor coordination problems. Sensory issues are also considered to feature in the condition. Typical features include:

1. Social interaction

The child with Asperger syndrome:

- will be socially isolated, but may not be worried about it;
- may become tense and distressed trying to cope with the approaches and social demands of others;
- begins to realise that his peers have friendships, particularly when he reaches adolescence. He may then want friends of his own, but lack strategies for developing and sustaining friendships;
- will find it difficult to pick up on social cues;
- may behave in a socially inappropriate way – singing along to songs from *Oliver!* is fine when you're listening to a CD, but embarrassing for your parents when you sing along during a performance in a West End theatre.

2. Social communication

The child with Asperger syndrome:

- may have superficially perfect spoken language, but it tends to be formal and pedantic. 'How do you do? My name is Jamie' may be a typical greeting from a teenager with Asperger syndrome, but it is one which sets him apart from his peers, marking him out for ridicule;
- often has a voice which lacks expression. He may also have difficulty in interpreting the different tones of voice of others. Most of us can tell if someone is angry, bored or delighted just from tone of voice. The child with Asperger syndrome often cannot make these judgements. This can lead to some tricky situations. One teacher had to give a student a pre-arranged visual signal: 'When I take my glasses off, you will know that I am cross with you.' Raising his voice had had no effect on the boy;

- may also have difficulty using and interpreting non-verbal communication such as body language, gesture and facial expression;

- may understand others in a very literal way. As Grandma dried four-year-old Ryan after his bath, she commented on his 'lovely bare feet'. Ryan became distressed and screamed, 'I'm not a bear!';

- fails to grasp the implied meanings of language. He would take a statement such as, 'It's hot in here' at face value, whereas the rest of us would take the hint and open a window.

3. Social imagination and flexibility of thought

The child with Asperger syndrome:

- often has an all-absorbing interest which his peers may find unusual;
- may insist that certain routines are adhered to;
- is limited in his ability to think and play creatively;
- struggles to adapt his behaviour appropriately to different situations;
- finds it difficult to draw inferences or use deductive thinking;
- finds it difficult to recognize and accept another's point of view;
- often has problems transferring skills from one setting to another.

4. Motor clumsiness

The child with Asperger syndrome:

- may be awkward and gauche in his movements;
- often has organisational problems – unable to find his way around or collect the equipment he needs;
- finds it hard to write and draw neatly, and often leaves tasks unfinished;
- struggles getting changed without help and organising movements in PE.

5. Sensory issues

The child with Asperger syndrome:

- may be hypersensitive or hyposensitive in each area of sensory functioning;
- may be hypersensitive and cover ears or hum loudly to block out noises such as squeaks on a blackboard or hyposensitive and try to create noise by running taps or similar;
- may overreact to strong or artificial light or, conversely, not be able to judge depth;
- may react to certain perfumes, food smells or toilet smells;
- may reject particular foods or textures, choosing bland foods or, conversely, seek out strong-tasting foods;
- may be unable to tolerate 'scratchy' clothing or labels in clothing or resist certain activities such as brushing teeth or having hair or nails cut. Hyposensitivity may lead to a lack of awareness of pain or feeling hot and cold;

- may have difficulties in fast-moving sports or PE activities such as doing somersaults and dressing and undressing. Hyposensitivity may lead to sensation-seeking, rocking, swinging or clumsiness;
- may have poor body awareness including poor posture, clumsiness and apparent low energy.

Case studies

Although children with Asperger syndrome have broad characteristics in common, the individual key features present in many different ways in different children. To illustrate this variety, here are six brief case studies of contrasting children. Sebastian and George are both infants, Alastair and Michael are juniors and Jeff and Adrian are at secondary school.

1. Sebastian

Sebastian, a solemn-faced five-year-old boy, already had a diagnosis of semantic-pragmatic disorder. On starting school, he immediately experienced difficulties:

- He showed little interest in the other children, simply intervening in their play in order to take over equipment such as the computer.
- He couldn't stay with a partner in PE or games, and at playtime he could be found 'chugging' round the circles marked on the playground, sounding like a train.
- He engaged in self-directed or ritualistic activities, especially switching lights on and off and activating the fire alarm and fire extinguishers.

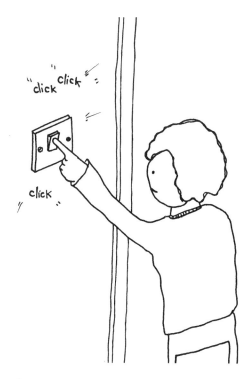

Figure 2.1 Sebastian flicking the lights on and off

- He constantly asked questions in a deep stentorian tone, often when he knew the answers already.
- He gave orders to adults – 'Get it NOW!' – but with no intention of being rude.
- When in the classroom, he often produced loud and uncontrolled noises which sounded like cars, whistles or bells.
- He didn't comply with his teacher's instructions.
- He ran out of the classroom and turned the taps on in the cloakroom.
- Any imaginative play was solitary and related to his special interests.
- There were some difficulties in PE, and he had had occupational therapy.

At home, Sebastian's Mum had noted his unusual preoccupations from an early age. They included shutting doors and flicking lights and a fascination for central heating pipes. He liked things to happen in a set order. For example, before he could eat a boiled egg, he had to check the egg timer and arrange a particular spoon, plate and egg-cup in a certain way on the table. He watched *Thomas the Tank Engine* videos endlessly.

2. George

George, six years old, was still in a reception class.

- A passive child, he had no interest in other children.
- He preferred to complete the same form board over and over again.
- Most of his peers gave up trying to interact with him.
- A few peers treated him cruelly. They threw a ball for him to retrieve like a dog and told him to lick the floor in the toilets; he saw no reason not to comply.
- He had bizarre language, especially when answering questions. He often echoed what had been said.
- He had some odd facial expressions which were unrelated to context.
- His reading and spelling were very good (for his age), but his comprehension was poor.
- He walked on tiptoe, flapping his hands and slapping his legs.
- He liked to have a small piece of string to 'twizzle'.
- He only ate mashed potato and vanilla ice cream. In fact, he only ate foods which were white.

3. Alastair

Alastair, nine years old, was relatively new to his school. His previous school had seen him as a deliberately uncooperative child with behavioural difficulties.

- He found interacting with other children very difficult.
- He wanted to have friends and would approach other children, but his approaches were clumsy – perhaps pushing or kicking someone. He was surprised and distressed at any retaliation.
- He was extremely sensitive to teasing, and felt he was the sole butt of teasing.
- He found it hard to understand instructions which were given to the whole class, but couldn't seem to ask for help.
- He had great difficulty following the rules of games such as rounders.
- He often said things which were out of the blue and unrelated to what was happening.
- He wanted his work to look perfect. He would keep rubbing a word out and writing it again until there was a hole in the paper.
- He was frequently tense and anxious, but unable to express his feelings.
- He found change unnerving.
- He forgot where things were stored in the classroom, even though he'd been in the same room for almost a year.

4. Michael

Michael, eight years old, was a Year 3 child in a Year 2 class.

- He wanted to involve others in his play, but he would grab them physically, rather than ask them to join him.
- His language sounded old fashioned; other children saw him as odd and mostly avoided him.
- He was unaware of the consequences of his actions on the feelings of others. Having tied string across the stairs, he was only interested in recording how many times his brother bumped his head on the way down, unaware that it might hurt him.
- He had excellent skills with construction toys, but would never let anyone share his play.
- He was particularly fascinated by electrical wiring, but was unaware of the dangers.
- The sound of the wind made him scream.

Figure 2.2 Michael had excellent skills with construction toys but would never let anyone join in his play

5. Jeff

Jeff, at age 14, was in Year 8 in an all-boys secondary school.

- He became very anxious at lunchtime at the prospect of going into the noisy, bustling dining hall.

- He didn't like to be watched while he was eating. Even at home, he would eat in his bedroom if visitors came.

- He watched the others to see what to do in group or team activities, but he always seemed out of step.

- He thought that others were picking on him, and overreacted by bringing a screwdriver to school to 'get them'.

- He would talk endlessly about agriculture if he could find anyone to listen.

- With poor coordination, he irritated the others in his PE class. Nobody wanted him on their team.

6. Alex

Alex, at 16 years old, had been a pupil in a residential school for children with speech and language difficulties. His speech therapist described him as 'an absent-minded professor'.

- The unwritten social rules were a closed book to Alex. He called to his teacher across the classroom 'She's got no idea!' in reference to his support assistant.

- In partner activities, he ignored his partner's attempts to work with him, sometimes pushing him away.

- He was very sensitive to name calling, but was seen as eccentric by the other boys (who made up a predictable nickname from Alex's surname).

- He had semantic-pragmatic language difficulties.

- He talked in a 'mid-Atlantic' accent, at high speed and full volume.

- He had comprehension difficulties, and he would question and interrupt inappropriately.

- He enjoyed talking about himself and his interests, including video games, watching TV, entering competitions, reading comics and using the computer.

- He had recently discovered jokes, and carried joke books around with him.

- He had unique strategies for solving maths questions. He became cross and confused by his teacher's attempts to teach him more regular strategies.

- He found problem solving difficult because he could not detect what strategy to apply.

- His body language was gauche, his gestures lacked in spontaneity and his range of facial expression was limited.

Assessment: background to current approaches

> We try not to stick the Asperger 'label' on him like a blob on the end of his nose.
>
> Lynda Bannister (Mother of John)

As with autism, no blood test or brain scan yet exists which can make a clear-cut diagnosis of Asperger syndrome, and children with Asperger syndrome cannot be distinguished by their physical appearance. Whilst it is accepted that autism is a development disorder of non-specific origin which is organically based and which has pervasive psychological effects, it can still only be recognised by informed observation of behaviour. It cannot be identified by a specific behaviour, rather it is inferred from the interpretation of a pattern of behaviours. This interpretation depends on a 'sound background of clinical knowledge', according to Uta Frith (1989), an eminent researcher in the field of autism and Asperger syndrome. Christopher Gillberg (Gillberg and Coleman 1992), who has carried out a great deal of research into the condition of Asperger syndrome, writes that 'clinical experience is a . . . fundamental element of utmost importance' in making a diagnosis and refers to experienced clinicians' 'gestalt acumen', which enables them to recognise the disorder despite widely varying individual presentation.

Digby Tantam (1997), a psychiatrist who has been particularly involved in the diagnosis of adolescents and adults with Asperger syndrome, encapsulates the particular difficulties in diagnosing the condition when he describes people with Asperger syndrome as 'more individual than individual'.

The above case studies serve to illustrate just how different individuals with Asperger syndrome can be from one another. Researchers have worked increasingly collaboratively to develop consistent criteria for the diagnosis of autism and Asperger syndrome. This has helped to clarify the boundaries of the conditions, but the debate continues.

A landmark in the search for diagnostic criteria which would be both necessary and sufficient to describe and specify autism came with Lorna Wing's identification of the 'triad of impairment' of social interaction in 1981. All aspects of the triad – impaired social interaction, impaired social communication and impaired play and lack of flexible thinking – combine to define autism as they are present in all those with autism but not present in this particular combination in other groups.

This definition formed the basis of the diagnostic criteria for autism in the World Classification Systems: *ICD 9* (WHO 1978) and *DSM III-R* (American Psychiatric Association 1987). Then in 1992, for the first time, *ICD 10* (WHO) gave diagnostic criteria for Asperger syndrome separately from autism. Diagnostic criteria were further refined in *DSM IV*, which is currently due for revision to result in *DSM V*. This may result in changes in the way the triad is defined. At the time of writing, however, criteria defining Asperger syndrome remain similar to those for autism, but without the language and cognitive impairments.

Diagnosis of Asperger syndrome should involve a range of professionals. Many professionals will contribute information relevant to identifying the child's difficulties, as will the parents.

Differential diagnosis

Differential diagnosis is the process of deciding what the condition is – and what it isn't. It involves comparing the child's behaviour with behaviour typical of other disorders which could account for the same symptoms. It is worth noting, however, that some conditions can and do coexist.

Jonathan Green (1990), a child and adolescent psychiatrist who has researched the nature of Asperger syndrome, outlines several areas for differential diagnosis. He points out that the differential diagnosis of children who may have Asperger syndrome involves considering alternative conditions in which some of the features are similar to those of the triad of impairments. Such features are discussed below.

Ordinary insensitivity

Asperger (1944) saw the condition as an extreme form of male intelligence, indicating that the characteristic social insensitivity was at the end of a continuum of normal behaviour. However, as Green (1990) points out, there is evidence that this is not the case. In studies comparing children with Asperger syndrome to other child psychiatry patients with social difficulties, only the Asperger syndrome group showed 'odd and bizarre speech, gesture and facial expression'.

Emotional disorder

Children with emotional difficulties, perhaps due to family and social circumstances, may present as unusually withdrawn and uncommunicative. However, they will usually respond more quickly to treatment and intervention (Green op. cit.).

Dyspraxia

Children with Asperger syndrome are often clumsy, with poorly developed fine motor and eye–hand coordination skills. Conversely, some children with severe dyspraxia also experience marked social problems. Therefore, differential diagnosis can be difficult in some cases, particularly with younger children. However, the distinction is important because children whose problems are fundamentally associated with dyspraxia will respond more readily to social skills-based intervention because of a relatively intact ability to form social relationships. They are also less rigid and obsessive in their interests than children with Asperger syndrome. In terms of educational intervention, there will be areas of similarity, but the priorities will be different. Equally, some children diagnosed with dyspraxia may go on to be given the additional diagnosis of Asperger syndrome.

Language disorder

The borders of developmental language disorders and autism can be difficult to define. When children are able to compensate for language difficulties by using gesture, facial expression, mime and signs, it will be clear that that the source of difficulty is language-based. However, as Rutter (1978) observed, some children present a mixed picture. Social, communicative and behavioural difficulties may be observed in young children with severe receptive language disorders as well as in young children with autism spectrum disorders. Collaboration between professionals involved in assessment (e.g. speech and language therapists, psychologists and paediatricians) is essential. As the child reaches school age, the picture usually becomes clearer.

Attention Deficit Hyperactivity Disorder (ADHD)

Young children with ADHD will evidence many behaviours which may also be present in Asperger syndrome. Such behaviours include: not seeming to listen when spoken to directly; not following through on instructions; experiencing difficulty organising tasks and activities; talking excessively; interrupting; and being easily distracted. Occasionally, young children of five or six years of age with Asperger syndrome may initially be diagnosed as having ADHD, possibly being prescribed medication and being given appropriate behavioural intervention. Usually in the case of ADHD, prescribed medication, together with appropriate behavioural and social skills intervention, will bring about rapid improvement in social functioning. If, however, social difficulties remain and are resistant to change, the differential diagnosis of Asperger syndrome may need to be considered. Occasionally both conditions may coexist.

Multidisciplinary assessment

It is evident that the multifaceted nature of the difficulties and impairments of Asperger syndrome requires involvement in diagnosis and intervention from a variety of professionals working within different services. The needs of both child and family will best be served by an awareness amongst all the professionals of the range of skills and expertise which may be useful to deploy at an early stage in the process of assessment and identification.

Approaches to assessment

Assessment of children where an Asperger syndrome diagnosis is under consideration should first and foremost be based on:

- a thorough knowledge of the autism spectrum, the triad of impairments and the nature of Asperger syndrome;
- a thorough understanding of psychological explanations for the underlying impairments of Asperger syndrome;
- an awareness of the extremely individual presentation of the characteristic impairments of Asperger syndrome;
- a knowledge of the diagnostic criteria for Asperger syndrome in *ICD 10* and *DSM IV*.

This background knowledge can then be used to prompt:

- careful and sensitive gathering of information;
- informed observation;
- selection of situation and context;
- staging of appropriate interactive events, selection of tasks and useful assessment procedures and materials.

These principles have been subsumed and developed within the recommendations of the National Autism Plan.

The National Autism Plan for Children (NAPC)

In recognition of the need for broad-based, multiperspective, multidisciplinary assessment and intervention for children and young people evidencing possible characteristics of the autism spectrum, the National Initiative for Autism Screening and Assessment (NIASA) report (2003) provides comprehensive guidelines for services. These guidelines are published as the NAPC.

Key recommendations of the NAPC include:

- development of assessment and care pathways;
- early assessment, diagnosis and intervention;
- identified multi-agency/disciplinary team of professionals with specialist skills in the autism spectrum;
- individuals appropriately skilled and experienced to lead in the autism spectrum in each contributing service;
- key worker to coordinate and route families through the pathway;
- overall multi-agency coordinating group to ensure the development of the pathway to assessment, diagnosis and intervention, identify training needs and resource requirements and review service provision;

- emphasis on joint working with families and sharing key information and reports on the child;
- timescales and a suggested framework for the pathway:
  - ○ General Developmental Assessment (GDA) should be completed within 13 weeks of referral and then, if needed, a Multi-Agency Assessment (MAA);
  - ○ from referral for MAA to written feedback and discussion with the family should take not more than 17 weeks.

Multi-Agency Assessment (MAA) components

MAA components include:

- review of existing understanding of child and family's needs;
- observation of the child in at least two social settings (e.g. home and preschool/school) as well as clinic-based assessment;
- autism-specific diagnostic developmental interview (e.g. DISCO);
- cognitive assessment/profile of strengths and weaknesses;
- assessment of communication skills;
- assessment of sensory needs;
- assessment of behaviour and mental health;
- assessment of family needs;
- assessment of physical development;
- assessment of adaptive skills.

Multi-agency 'core team'

The multi-agency 'core team' would normally involve:

- specialist paediatrician (or child and adolescent psychiatrist);
- specialist speech and language therapist;
- educational and/or clinical psychologist;
- teacher or education specialist.

Additional involvement may be required, for example, from:

- occupational therapist;
- physiotherapist.

Multi-Agency Assessment (MAA) outcomes

- A coordinated care plan should be provided within six weeks of the MAA. The family should be given information about education, training, support services and local groups.
- Needs should be identified and addressed even if diagnosis is not given within the 17-week timeframe.

- The NAPC makes recommendations and interventions based on evidence that targeted intervention should begin as early as possible.
- IEP should be set up by an autism spectrum-trained teacher in conjunction with parents and professionals at home, school or nursery within six weeks of diagnosis.
- Interventions should be informed by specific autism spectrum expertise.

Autism spectrum pathways: developments

Nationally, there is great variability of the models of service currently offered. Although, multi-agency professionals are coming together to try to implement the NAPC plan across the country. Groups collaborating usually include paediatricians, speech and language therapists, educational and clinical psychologists and psychiatrists.

Most pathways are using clinically-based history together with observation of child – frequently Diagnostic Interview for Social and Communication Disorders (DISCO) or Autism Diagnostic Interview (ADI) and Autism Diagnostic Observation Schedule (ADOS). A range of appropriate interventions are being provided, including Early Bird, Early Bird Plus, Cygnet, Hanen, Picture Exchange Communication System (PECS) and Portage, school-based intervention, speech and language therapy and social skills groups. Most services recognise that the capacity to provide follow-up to assessment and diagnosis is limited. There are many examples, however, of the use of ingenuity and a high level of commitment from professionals to support children and their families.

Diagnostic and assessment tools for use within the autism spectrum

In the process of assessment, rating scales developed for use with children with autism spectrum disorders may be used. The following are some examples of rating scales.

Diagnostic Interview for Social and Communication Disorders (DISCO)

The DISCO schedule is a semi-structured interview developed by Dr Lorna Wing and Dr Judith Gould for use with children and adults who have difficulties with social interaction and/or communication. Information is systematically collected during an extensive interview with the parent and/or caregiver to compile a full history and a description of current functioning, including level of development in everyday skills and patterns of behaviour. The findings enable a clinical diagnosis to be made of disorders within the autistic spectrum and other disorders affecting social interaction and communication.

Diagnostic classification can be made according to established systems including *DSM IV* and *ICD 10*. Training is required to use DISCO (and is provided by Wing, Gould and colleagues at Elliot House Centre for Social and Communication Disorders in Bromley, Kent).

Autism Diagnostic Interview (ADI) (Le Couteur *et al.* 1989)

The ADI is a standardised interview originally developed as a research tool for use with parents. The areas of the triad are given extremely detailed coverage, and care is taken to present open-ended questions and probes for information which do not bias the answers elicited. An algorithm is provided to aid diagnosis for those using this procedure.

Autism Diagnostic Observation Schedule (ADOS) (Lord, Rutter, DiLavore and Risi 1999)

ADOS is a semi-structured, standardised assessment of communication, social interaction and play or imaginative use of materials. ADOS enables structured observations of social behaviour and communication to be made. Standard tasks and activities which invite participation in social interchanges are presented over a period of 30 to 45 minutes. Ratings made by the examiner contribute to a diagnostic algorithm. There are definitive threshold scores which establish a diagnosis against *DSM IV* and *ICD 10* criteria. However, the ADOS provides information on current behaviour only and is based on a limited true-sample. Therefore, it is recommended for use as one element of a comprehensive assessment which includes a diagnostic interview, observation across settings and other assessments. Training is required to administer the ADOS.

Gilliam Autism Rating Scale (GARS) (Gilliam 2003)

GARS is a behavioural checklist which may be used to help identify autism. The author stresses that full assessment should be carried out by a multi-disciplinary team. The scale comprises 42 items divided into three subtests; 14 additional items elicit information from parents about development during the first three years of childhood. The scale can be completed within ten minutes by parents and professionals at school and home. Standard scores and percentiles are provided together with a table which determines the likelihood of autism and indicates the degree of severity. While the GARS can be given by parents, teachers and other educationalists, the author stresses that the professional involved must have experience in testing and appraisal as well as training in psychometrics in order to interpret and use the test results.

The Childhood Autism Rating Scale (CARS) (Schopler *et al.* 1980)

CARS is a rating scale devised in North Carolina for use in the Treatment and Education of Autistic and Communication-Handicapped Children (TEACCH) clinic. It relies on a comprehensive set of observations based on several diagnostic systems. Evidence is gained for all 15 items which reflect many facts of autism. The rating scale is summative.

Children's Communication Checklist (CCC-2) (Bishop 2003)

CCC-2 is the most recent version of a checklist devised by Dr Dorothy Bishop in order to assess aspects of communicative impairment which she considers could not be adequately evaluated by other existing standardised language tests.

The 70-item questionnaire is completed by the parent or carer concerned about the communication skills of children aged between four and 16 years. Standard scores and percentiles can then be given for each of ten separate scales: speech; syntax; semantics; coherence; appropriate initiation; stereotyped language; use of context; non-verbal communication; social relations; and interests. This then leads to two composite scores:

- The General Communication Composite (GCC), which is used to identify children likely to have significant communication difficulties;
- The Social Interaction Deviance Composite (SIDC), which can give an indication of those children with a communication profile characteristic of autism.

The Psychoeducational Profile – Revised (PEP-R) (Schopler *et al.* 1990)

PEP-R involves presenting the child with a series of activities covering an inventory of behaviours and skills relevant to autism. It is designed to identify uneven and idiosyncratic learning patterns. Developmental skills are assessed in seven areas, and atypical behaviours are assessed in a further four areas. The resulting profile is used to help design individual education programmes for children.

The above instruments are reliable in discriminating children with autism from both those with severe learning difficulties and normally developing children from the age of three years onwards. However, these instruments are less sensitive in areas where the finest discrimination is required, for example in differentiating language disorders or mild Asperger syndrome. As yet, there is no established rating scale for use specifically with children suspected of having Asperger syndrome.

Leiter International Performance Scale Revised (Leiter-R) (Roid and Miller 1997)

Leiter-R, developed by Roid and Miller, is a non-verbal measure of cognitive ability. It can be used with children and young people between the ages of two to 21 years. There is no requirement to read, write or even speak, and instructions can be gestured.

The scales assess skills in two distinct domains:

- Attention & Memory;
- Visualisation & Reasoning.

In addition, an overall standardised score is obtainable.

In the authors' experience, the brightly coloured, logically presented, pictorial materials are very attractive to children and young people on the autism spectrum, who find the activities very accessible.

Qualitative assessment

While diagnostic and assessment tools such as these are useful, qualitative assessment remains crucial in the identification of Asperger syndrome, and in detailing the special educational needs which arise from it.

Such assessment takes account of functioning in and examining the interface between the areas of:

- social interaction;
- social communication;
- social imagination, flexible thinking and play;
- cognitive ability;

- sensory sensitivity;
- developmental skills in areas such as attention control, language levels, fine- and gross-motor functioning and independence skills.

Assessment should also always include:

- a thorough developmental history;
- background medical information;
- information from any therapeutic intervention undertaken;
- educational history;
- current educational attainments.

Assessment should include information from and observation across a range of settings, including the child's home, where possible. Assessment should be carried out over a period of time since behaviour can vary from day to day as well as in different settings and with different people.

Teaching contribution to assessment and diagnosis in Asperger syndrome

While it would be inappropriate for teachers to go solo in identifying, assessing or offering a diagnosis of Asperger syndrome for a child in the educational setting, the class teacher has an important role to play in the assessment process. Frequently, it is the teacher who is the first to notice behaviour which may seem odd, unusual or different compared to that of peers. The child may be placed at School Action within the graduated response outlined in the Special Educational Needs (SEN) Code of Practice and an Individual Education Plan (IEP) will need to be drawn up. At School Action Plus, collaboration with external agencies may lead to a request for more specialist information, for example, from the educational psychologist. If formal assessment of the child's special educational needs is undertaken, teaching staff will be expected to provide educational advice on the child.

In addition to the usual information collated on a child's educational attainments and his response to teaching, it will be helpful if the teacher gathers information regarding the child's functioning, skill levels and aspects of behaviour in areas which are particularly relevant to the assessment and diagnosis of Asperger syndrome (i.e. in the areas of social interaction, social communication, social imagination and flexible thinking and any other associated difficulties).

Social interaction

Assessment of social interaction involves judging the extent to which the child is able to:

- use gesture, body posture, facial expression and eye-to-eye gaze in one-to-one and group interaction (e.g. standing an appropriate distance away from others);
- appreciate social cues given by adults or children in one-to-one or large group conditions;
- develop peer friendships (Does the child play alone or have some ability to initiate or respond to interaction?);

- share an activity with other children or adults;
- seek comfort or affection when distressed, or offer comfort to others;
- share in others' enjoyment and pleasure;
- show different responses to different people and in different settings;
- imitate other children and adults;
- respond to social praise or criticism.

Social communication

Assessment of social communication involves judging the extent to which the child is able to:

- respond when called by name;
- follow verbal instructions in one-to-one situations or in small or large groups;
- take turns in conversation;
- initiate conversation, change topics and maintain an appropriate topic;
- be aware of the listener's needs and give non-verbal signals that he is listening;
- change topic and style of conversation to suit the listener;
- vary the tone and projection of voice according to the situation;
- recognise and respond to non-verbal cues (e.g. raised eyebrows and smile);
- understand implied meanings;
- tell or write an imaginative story;
- give a sequence of events or tell a simple story;
- give simple, ordered instructions.

Social imagination and flexible thinking

Assessment of social imagination and flexible thinking involves judging the extent to which the child is able to:

- have a range of interests and an ability to share them (as opposed to having all-absorbing, exclusive interests);
- change his behaviour according to the situation;
- accept changes in routines, rules or procedures;
- play imaginatively, alone or cooperatively;
- accept others' points of view;
- generalise learning or generate skills across the curriculum;
- plan (e.g. assembling equipment and sorting out the steps of a task);
- suggest possible explanations of events;
- use inference and deduction in an academic or social context.

Observation should be carried out in a range of settings, including informal and non-academic contexts such as:

- Playtime, lunch breaks, noting:
  - the extent to which their play is solitary;
  - whether they seem anxious when others approach them;
  - their level of cooperative/imaginative play.

- Cloakrooms, arrivals and departures, noting:
  - how they leave or greet their parent/carer/teacher/peers;
  - their self-help/independence skills.

- PE, noting:
  - their ability to get changed independently;
  - how well they find and work with a partner;
  - their level of participation in team games;
  - their motor and coordination skills.

- Class performances (e.g. Harvest Festival and class assembly), noting:
  - their ability to take on a role;
  - their ability to project their voice for the audience;
  - their ability to take turns;
  - their ability to wait and listen to others.

Additional opportunities for observation will present themselves during classroom activities. The use of the questionnaire in Chapter 6 will help in both forming an assessment of the child's functioning, including motor skills and sensory sensitivities, and devising individual teaching programmes.

Summary

- There is no simple test, marker or checklist which will confirm the diagnosis of Asperger syndrome.
- The presence of Asperger syndrome is inferred on the basis of interpretation of a pattern of behaviours.
- The 'boundaries' of Asperger syndrome overlap other conditions, and an awareness of the issues of differential diagnosis is essential.
- Adequate assessment and diagnosis of Asperger syndrome will involve a range of professionals from various disciplines.
- Teachers and educational support staff can provide vital and specific information to aid in the assessment process.
- Specialised tools exist which may help in the assessment process, but the role of qualitative, observation-based assessment is crucial.

Educational implications of current theories

As educationalists, it is our responsibility in teaching children to:

- recognise patterns of strengths and weaknesses;
- build upon strengths;
- generate effective intervention strategies.

How are we to do this for the child with Asperger syndrome?

In recent years, in the wake of the 1978 Warnock Report and the 1981, 1993 and 1996 Education Acts, there has been a movement away from 'labelling' children and, therefore, from paying much attention to a child's 'diagnosis' when planning intervention. The behaviourist school of thought has also promoted an emphasis on intervention at the level of observable behaviours and consequences.

In our experience with children with Asperger syndrome however, we have found that the label or diagnosis is crucial.

In order to provide effective education for children with Asperger syndrome, it is essential to understand the nature of the impairments, sources of the difficulties and areas of strength – in effect, the cognitive style.

To attempt to alter and modify individual behaviours in a piecemeal fashion with children with Asperger syndrome is a strategy which has major shortcomings. This is the stage we were at in the teaching of children with autism until relatively recently. There was recognition that autism is an organically-based disorder characterised by a range of identifiable behaviours. The missing link was at the level of psychological functioning.

The shift in emphasis in our understanding of the nature of the difficulties in autism occurred as the triad of impairments was identified, pinpointing the underlying social deficit. Previously, the difficulties of language and behaviour in autism were assumed to cause the social difficulties. Now, the difficulty in social interaction and understanding is seen to both underpin the difficulty in communication and cause many of the difficulties in behaviour.

The effort to explain the sources of social difficulty at the psychological level has led to a number of powerful models of the child's psychological functioning. These models are powerful in their ability to generate approaches to assessment and intervention.

The 'Theory of Mind' impairment and 'Mindblindness'

An ability we all appear to have, which is so commonplace as to have escaped specific investigation until relatively recently, is the ability to think about other people's thinking and, further, to think about what they think about our thinking and, even further, to think about what they think we think about their thinking, and so on. This ability underlies much of our interaction with others, informing our understanding of others' behaviour and influencing our actions towards others.

In psychological terms, this is described as the ability to appreciate that other people have mental states (i.e. intentions, needs, desires and beliefs) which may be different from our own. The term given to this ability is 'Theory of Mind'.

In 1985, a group of research psychologists (Baron-Cohen, Leslie and Frith) proposed that people with autism lack a 'Theory of Mind'. In 1990, Simon Baron-Cohen went on to describe this as a form of 'Mindblindness'. It was suggested that this basic cognitive deficit in autism constrains children to a deviant path of development and that this, in turn, gives rise to complex surface behaviours.

The experiment designed to reveal the characteristic deficits of Theory of Mind in autism is now quite famous and is known as 'The Sally/Anne test'. It was designed by Baron-Cohen in 1985 to test the prediction that children with autism lack the ability to understand beliefs.

The experiment was carried out:

- with children with autism with mental ages above four years;
- with a control group of children with Down syndrome who also had mental ages above four years;
- with normally developing four-year-old children.

In the Sally/Anne test, Sally and Anne are two dolls. Sally has a basket and Anne has a box. In the story, which is acted out in front of the child, Sally puts a marble into her basket while Anne is watching. She then leaves to go for a walk. While she is away, Anne puts Sally's marble into her own box. Sally returns from her walk and wants to play with her marble. The child subject is then asked, 'Where will Sally look for her marble?'. The correct answer is 'In her basket', for that is where Sally left her marble and where she believes it still is. Children with autism answer that Sally will look 'In the box' because that is where the marble actually is – even though Sally has not seen Anne take it from the basket and place it in the box. This contrasts with the children in the control groups who give the correct answer.

Many further experiments have been carried out in order to examine this area of functioning. The evidence is that whereas most young children can pass this sort of test by the age of four years, even the more able children on the autism spectrum do not master the task until a later age. Uta Frith (1991) tested 50 able children on the autism spectrum and found that no child passed Theory of Mind tasks with a chronological age of under 11 years and a mental age of under five years.

In children with Asperger syndrome, Theory of Mind still constitutes an area of difficulty. The more able children do come to an understanding, although at a much later stage than in the normally developing child. Happé and Frith (1995) suggest that this happens between the ages of nine and 14 years, in contrast to four years in normal development.

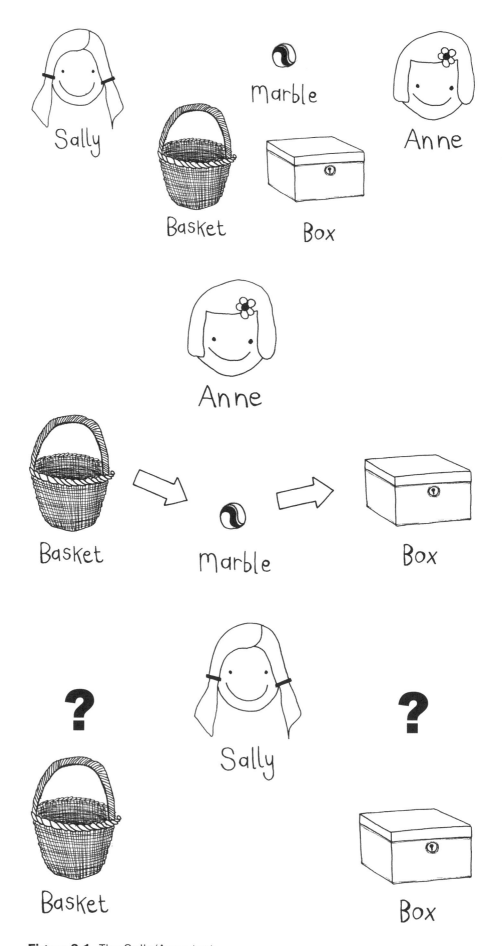

Figure 3.1 The Sally/Anne test

It appears that the route to developing an understanding of other minds, and even an awareness that other people do have minds, is much more difficult for people with Asperger syndrome. It can be likened, in degree of severity, to the difficulties involved in a dyslexic child learning to read. In contrast, for the rest of us it is so effortless that we feel that we were born with it. Even when a basic level of understanding is reached, the young person with Asperger syndrome may not manage to reach the next stage of understanding, which is that people not only have thoughts and feelings, but they can reflect on these (i.e. have thoughts and feelings about their own and other people's thoughts and feelings).

The ability of children with Asperger syndrome to perform the Theory of Mind task can be investigated in practical situations in the classroom. An alternative experiment to the Sally/Anne test which can easily be replicated is the Smarties test (Perner *et al.* 1989). In this test, the child is shown a Smarties tube and asked what he thinks it contains. Upon answering 'Smarties', the child is then shown the contents of the tube: a pencil. He is then asked what another child will say if shown the tube and asked the same question. Typically, the child with Asperger syndrome will answer, 'A pencil'. Even when the next child is brought in and gets the answer wrong, the child with Asperger syndrome will fail to see the point or the joke, as it were. This procedure can be adapted using ordinary classroom materials. For example, out of the child's view, a familiar crayon tub is emptied, the crayons are replaced by lego bricks and questions are asked as above.

Implications of the 'Theory of Mind' impairment

The effects of the 'Theory of Mind' impairment in children with Asperger syndrome are pervasive, subtle and specific. Jordan and Powell (1995) highlight the implications of this impairment. Difficulties as they are presented in Asperger syndrome include:

- **Difficulty in predicting others' behaviour, leading to a fear and avoidance of other people.** Thus there will be a preference for activities which do not depend on other people or even require the involvement of others.

- **Difficulty in reading the intentions of others and understanding the motives behind their behaviour.** Oliver, a young teenager, was quite willing (when prompted by other boys) to type out salacious remarks on the school word processor. He circulated copies and even read them out to the teacher. He was so pleased to have the boys' attention and be able to make them laugh. He thought they were now his friends.

- **Difficulty in explaining their own behaviour.** Lukas, a young man in a school for children with emotional and behavioural difficulties, alleged that a teacher had assaulted him, deliberately pushing him into a pile of chairs. He failed to say that he had been balanced on the back of a chair himself at the time, refusing to climb down and pushing the teacher away from him. When this was pointed out, he protested indignantly, 'It was obvious, it was obvious!'.

- **Difficulty in understanding emotions – their own and those of others – leading to a lack of empathy.** Jake, a primary school child, would cry if he was upset, but would then try to push the tears back in; he was confused by his own feelings. Craig, in an infant language unit, stopped in the middle of a tearful outburst to squint at the tears glistening on his lashes, his attention caught by this strange phenomenon.

Mahmoud was a teenager who was developing some awareness of his difficulties. When upset and angry he would run to his support assistant saying, 'Tell me what I'm feeling, tell me, tell me!'.

- **Difficulty understanding that behaviour affects how others think or feel, leading to a lack of conscience or motivation to please.** Michael used to tie string across the staircase for his brother to trip over. He was unaware of the pain and injury this could cause; he just wanted to count how many times the brother bumped his head on the way down. In the classroom, the child with Asperger syndrome does not pick up the idea of paying attention to the teacher when she is speaking – or at least pretending to – as most children do in order to conform to teacher expectations.

- **Difficulty taking into account what other people know or can be expected to know, leading to pedantic or incomprehensible language.** When the child with Asperger syndrome speaks, either no background information is given, so that the listener has no idea of what the subject of the conversation is, or every detail is given to the point of boring the listener completely.

- **Inability to read and react to the listener's level of interest in what is being said.** An obsessive interest may be talked about endlessly. Alex, at the age of 16, had recently discovered jokes. He carried several joke books around in his bag, reading out jokes repeatedly, regardless of the listener's mood or interest.

- **Inability to anticipate what others might think of one's actions.** Derek had just started at secondary school and had gone to the Baths with his class. He found that his swimming trunks were inside out. He went into the public area to ask his teacher for help, unaware of the effect of his nakedness on those around him.

- **Inability to deceive or to understand deception.** A teacher came into the classroom to find that someone played a prank and hidden the chalk. She asked who did it. Martin told her the culprit's name without hesitation.

- **No sharing of attention, leading to idiosyncratic reference.** A teacher, leading a group activity in an infant class, held up a picture of a farmyard. The focus of all the children was on the different farm animals – except for one child's focus. Marcus, who was fascinated by electricity pylons, noticed a tiny pylon in the background of the picture and could focus on nothing else.

- **Lack of understanding of social interaction, leading to difficulties with taking turns, poor topic maintenance in conversation and inappropriate use of eye contact.** Marco observed the frequency of eye contact amongst other people and asked, 'Why do people pass messages with their eyes?'

- **Difficulty in understanding pretending and differentiating fact from fiction.** A diligent teacher and support assistant spent two years teaching Aaron, an able junior school pupil, the nature of stories. Eventually, the penny dropped: 'Oh! You mean it's not true!'

All of these difficulties which arise from the Theory of Mind impairment affect the child's ability to interact socially in the classroom and in the wider school environment. They influence not only his behaviour, but also his thinking and thus his ability to benefit from the school curriculum.

'Theory of Mind' developments: the role of emotion and the sense of self

Hobson (1993) believes the difficulties associated with 'Theory of Mind' originate at a much earlier stage in development. He holds that human capacities for social interaction are based on certain innate abilities. Difficulties in Theory of Mind, he postulates, arise from the infant's 'lack of basic perceptual-affective abilities and propensities that are required for a person to engage in "personal relatedness with others"'. In order for intersubjective understanding to begin at all, infants have to have an ability to respond naturally with feelings to the feelings, expressions, gestures and actions of others. They must have biologically given, 'prewired' capacities for direct perception of others' emotions and attitudes in order to begin to develop an understanding of others as separate beings with their own feelings, thoughts, beliefs and attitudes. And also, of course, to recognise themselves as beings with feelings, thoughts, beliefs and attitudes. They must also realise that there is common ground, though each of us views it from a different angle.

The concept of a person is 'logically prior to that of an individual consciousness' and it is this concept, Hobson (1993) argues, which is missing in autism.

Several other theorists have suggested related explanations for the difficulties in autism. Most notable in terms of educational implications is Jordan and Powell (1995), who propose that the difficulties in autism might derive from the failure to develop 'an experiencing self'. They note that children with autism have difficulties in developing a personal memory for events (i.e. personal episodic memory). That is, they have difficulty in experiencing events subjectively and then in being able to recall these events without effort – an ability most of us take for granted. When we wish to recall an event, we tend to ask ourselves, 'What was I doing? Where was I? Who was with me?'. Ironically, although children with Asperger syndrome are often described as egocentric, real egocentricity as we understand it in our non-autistic day-to-day lives, seems to be lacking.

The implication for teachers of this lack of a sense of experiencing self is that the child will need a structure which will cue him into the salient points. The child's role in the learning process will need to be highlighted, drawn to his attention visually and verbally as Powell and Jordan (1997) suggest, using photographs, videos and prompt scripts. They point to the interrelatedness of emotions and thinking in normal development which leads us to attach 'meaning' to events. Without this personally experienced meaningfulness of events, children with autistic difficulties learn 'from the outside in', as it were, by rote and mechanistically.

The challenge to teaching presented by Powell and Jordan is that of explicit teaching of meaning; the child's attention must be explicitly drawn to how new information affects the way in which he understands the world. In this sense, transfer of knowledge becomes a process that needs to be directly taught rather than assumed.

Principles of intervention: teaching points

Teachers and others working with children with Asperger syndrome need to be aware of the following points:

- Dealing with surface behaviours is not enough to correct fundamental deficits.
- It is difficult to teach levels of social and personal awareness that we ourselves did not have to similarly learn.

- Learning the social skills necessary for the classroom and playground is an extremely demanding and stressful task for the child with Asperger syndrome. There may not be much space left for dealing with academic tasks. Conversely, academic tasks may provide relief from the stress of social interaction.

- There is a need to specifically teach the basic social skills of listening and not interrupting, pausing to allow others a turn, sharing equipment, waiting in lines and working in small groups.

- The child needs help to recognise the effects of his actions on others and to change his behaviour accordingly.

- Beware of assuming that the child's level of spoken language represents his communication level. It is necessary to check the child's understanding.

- Be explicit when giving instructions. Don't assume that the context will help to make the meaning clear.

- Assess the child's ability to use language socially. Specifically teach such skills as initiating a dialogue, listening to replies and following up with an appropriate response.

- Strategies to develop the child's self-concept, self-image and self-reference need to be built in.

- Teach the child to identify emotions as physical, visual and auditory expressions, but also in situ, drawing attention to the emotional expressions of others.

- Ensure that the child is giving attention to the topic, subject or activity which is meant to be the focus of attention.

- Alert the child to his role in tasks, situations and events; use strategies to prompt the development of a personal memory.

- Beware of assuming that the 'meaning' of any task, situation, activity or event is clear to the child; relate the meaning, where possible, to the perspective he is taking.

- Draw the child's attention to the use of gesture, facial expression, eye direction and proximity in social interaction to convey attitudes and meaning.

- Make the child aware of himself as a problem solver, using visual and auditory means to promote self-reflection and recognition of self-experience.

- Don't assume the child will be able to read your intentions from your behaviour.

- The child needs to learn that other people have feelings, thoughts, beliefs and attitudes and to become aware of his own thinking, feelings, beliefs and attitudes.

- Teach pretending and help the child discriminate between pretence and reality.

Central Coherence Deficit

Central Coherence Deficit is another theory put forward to account for the impairments in autism. Uta Frith, in 1989, suggested that some aspects of functioning in autism cannot be explained by Theory of Mind impairment alone (e.g. the insistence on sameness, attention to detail rather than the whole, insistence on routine, obsessive preoccupations and the existence of special skills).

Frith's research findings indicated that children on the autism spectrum performed better than would be expected on the Children's Embedded Figures Test (CEFT) and on the Block Design Test, which is a sub-test of the Wechsler Intelligence Scales for Children (WISC) (Wechsler 1991). The CEFT (Witkin *et al.* 1971) involves spotting a hidden figure (e.g. a triangle in a larger drawing of a pram). The Block Design Test requires the child to assemble individual segmented blocks to match a given drawing of a whole, which involves first breaking up the whole design into its constituent parts.

Frith argued that in autism, the problem with these tasks was not in overcoming the tendency to see the picture as a whole, but in the failure to see the whole picture in the first place. The advantage shown by children on the autism spectrum is thus attributed specifically to their ability to see parts over wholes. Interestingly, as Francesca Happé (1994) points out, Leo Kanner, in 1943, saw as one of the universal features of autism the 'inability to experience wholes without full attention to the constituent parts'. He also commented on the tendency to fragmentary processing and the children's resistance to change: 'a situation, a performance, a sentence is not regarded as complete if it is not made up of exactly the same elements that were present at the time the child was first confronted with it'.

Frith (1989) describes 'central coherence' as the tendency to draw together diverse information to construct higher-level meaning in context. In individuals who process information normally, there is a tendency to make sense of situations and events according to their context. In individuals with Asperger syndrome this does not occur.

Five-year-old Ben, sitting in the interview room with his reading folder on his knee, was asked by the psychologist to 'take your book out'. He got up and left the room with it. Ben later read a whole story involving grumbling children taking all their old toys to a jumble sale at their parents' instruction. Subsequently, given their pocket money, the children buy back all their toys, arriving home to their parents' looks of consternation. Ben completely missed the point of the story, even though he could identify the pictures in which the children and the parents looked sad or happy and relate what happened to the toys. He showed real interest, though, in the appearance of a drawing of a fan in the corner of several of the pictures. (When Ryan protested, 'I'm not a bear!' to his grandmother's comment on his 'lovely bare feet', he made a similar mistake.)

Implications of the Central Coherence Deficit

Some of the difficulties which can be expected to occur when there is difficulty recognising wholes and in making sense of events in context and preference for detail include:

- **Idiosyncratic focus of attention**. The child will not necessarily focus on what the teacher may consider to be the obvious focus of attention or point of the task.

- **Imposition of own perspective**. What appears prominent to the child will determine his perspective on the learning situation. William was fascinated by knights and castles. His teacher led a group discussion on the topic of faces, and gave him collage materials to construct a face picture. William used the pieces to assemble a picture of a castle!

- **Preference for the known**. Without the ability to quickly see the point, and get the drift of others' actions and communications, the child with Asperger syndrome will feel safer sticking to known procedures and established routines.

- **Inattentiveness to new tasks**. The teacher will find it difficult to enthuse a pupil with Asperger syndrome by talking of new, exciting and interesting ideas as their potential appeal will not be recognised.

- **Difficulty in choosing and prioritising**. Without a guiding principle or super-ordinate goal, the child with Asperger syndrome will have difficulty in choosing and prioritising. Jake, when asked to choose the sweets he wanted, constructed a complex chart that listed categories of sweets and brand names before he could decide whether to have Rolos, Wine Gums or Polo Mints.

- **Difficulty in organising self, materials, experiences**. Again, without a guiding principle or overall plan, the child with Asperger syndrome will often have difficulty in all matters of organisation. He may be unable to find the art paper in a familiar classroom, find his way round school in time for the next lesson or equip his school bag with the books and pens he is likely to need. In fact, the school bag has, on more than one occasion, been kicked and blamed for not yielding up its contents more efficiently.

- **Difficulty seeing connections and generalising skills and knowledge**. Children with Asperger syndrome may show great aptitude in one area of knowledge, but will be unable to generalise this in a variety of situations. Clyde has tremendous ability in maths and is able to calculate three-figure multiplication in his head at age nine years. However, when his teacher gave the class a test involving different presen-tations of the sums, Clyde became angry and anxious, crying, 'You didn't teach me these, I can't do them.'

- **Lack of compliance**. For the teacher with a class of 30 or more children, this is probably the most taxing aspect of this difficulty. Aidan spent the first two years of his schooling wandering about the classroom and school at will and talking at length in an American accent (though both his parents had broad Lancashire accents), seemingly unaware of the requirement to stay with his class group. He baffled his teachers with his apparent insouciance.

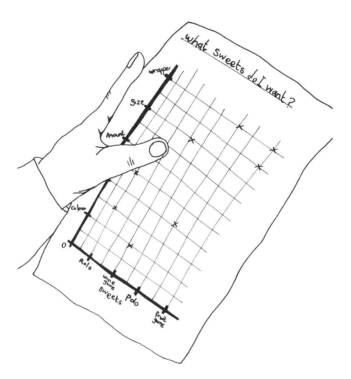

Figure 3.2 Difficulties choosing

Again, all of these difficulties which arise from the proposed Central Coherence Deficit affect the child's ability to integrate into his class group in school. They restrict the child's ability to cooperate with, or even, simply, to notice the demands of others. They affect not only behaviour, but also thinking, and thus the ability to benefit from the school curriculum.

Principles of intervention: teaching points

Teachers and others working with children with Asperger syndrome need to be aware of the following points:

- Make the beginning and end points of tasks clear (e.g. using a list of steps to task completion or a series of prompt cards, pictures or diagrams).
- Consider using a model or picture of the final goal or end product so that the child knows what is expected.
- Avoid ambiguity; use visual clues to highlight meaning.
- Specifically teach the child how to make choices.
- Build in opportunities for the child to generalise knowledge and skills.
- Make the connections with previous skills or knowledge explicit.
- Teach stories using sequences of picture cards. Draw the child's attention to cause and effect and motives and plot.

Executive Function Deficit

Executive function is defined as 'the ability to maintain an appropriate problem-solving set for attainment of a future goal' (Luria 1966). Sally Ozonoff gives this definition in her 1995 paper, proposing deficits in executive functioning as the central deficit in autism. Executive functioning is mediated by the frontal lobes of the brain. One hypothesis is that this area of the brain guides behaviour by mental representations or 'inner models of reality' (Goldman-Rakic 1987).

Executive function behaviours include:

- planning;
- self-monitoring;
- inhibition of prepotent, correct responses;
- behavioural flexibility;
- organised search;
- set maintenance and change.

Ozonoff points out how these functions are often impaired in people with autism and Asperger syndrome. The behaviour of people with autism is often rigid, inflexible and perseverative. They are often impulsive and have difficulty holding back a response. They may have a large store of knowledge, but have trouble applying this knowledge meaningfully. They often seem narrowly focused on detail, and cannot see the whole picture.

Implications of Executive Function Deficit

Some of the implications of Executive Function Deficit include:

- **Difficulties in perceiving emotion**. There is an inability to hold images of the different forms of expression internally. The person with autism or Asperger syndrome is guided by the external appearance of the face or the perceptual pattern, so that an open mouth can equally be an expression of fear or surprise. (The perceptual pattern thus dominating and determining the response is described as 'prepotent'.)

- **Difficulties in imitation**. Similarly, there is a need to hold an image of the other's behaviour in mind long enough to be able to imitate it.

- **Difficulties in pretend play**. In order to pretend, external objects in the environment have to be held in mind, then transformed or re-presented as something else.

The difficulty with Executive Function Deficit theory as a primary explanation of autism impairments is that children with other developmental difficulties (e.g. attention deficit disorder and conduct disorder) also evidence executive function impairments.

However, the implications in terms of the children's behaviour may include:

- **Difficulty in planning**. Children with Asperger syndrome often appear incapable of organising an approach to a task. Alan had been in the same classroom for nearly a year, but when asked to go and get some paper, he meandered into the centre of the classroom then stood, looking lost. Craig, in the nursery for 18 months, was asked to hand round the biscuits. He could not see where to start and how to get from one table to another. When he got to the second table (where his own seat was), he sat down, took a biscuit for himself and ate it.

- **Difficulty in starting and stopping**. Very often, the child with Asperger syndrome sits at the desk or table with all his work in front of him, but seemingly is unable or unwilling to start the task. A little help getting started, perhaps a physical prompt, is often all that is necessary. Once he gets going, however, he may perseverate, unclear as to when the task is finished.

Principles of intervention: teaching points

Teachers and others working with children with Asperger syndrome need to be aware of the following points:

- break tasks down into clearly identifiable steps;
- develop a hierarchy of sub-goals;
- sequence activities towards the goals.

To enable the child to consolidate and apply knowledge, the child will need help to:

- identify the main idea in new information;
- draw associations between new knowledge and already acquired knowledge;
- see the whole picture rather than focus on details.

Summary

Before planning educational intervention for the child with Asperger syndrome, it is important to understand the child at the psychological level.

Current psychological theories which extend our understanding of children with autism and Asperger syndrome propose that these children have impairments in Theory of Mind as well as Central Coherence Deficit and Executive Function Deficit. An understanding of these theories leads to an understanding of their educational implications.

A framework for educational intervention

Recent legislation and governmental guidance has established a changing educational context which is increasingly conducive to meeting the needs of individual children on the autism spectrum.

Recent initiatives include:

- Every Child Matters (2003);
- Good Practice Guidance (2002);
- National Curriculum amendments (2008);
- Inclusion Development Programme (IDP) (2009);
- Disability Discrimination Act (1995);
- The Autism Education Trust (AET) (established 2007).

Every Child Matters (2003)

Launched in 2003, Every Child Matters is the Government agenda for bringing about change for children. It outlines 5 key outcomes, stating that every child, whatever their background or circumstances, should have the support they need to:

- be healthy (enjoy good physical and mental health and living a healthy lifestyle);
- stay safe (be protected from harm and neglect);
- enjoy and achieve (get the most out of life and developing the skills for adulthood);
- make a positive contribution (be involved with the community and society and not engaging in anti-social or offending behaviour);
- achieve economic well-being (not be prevented by economic disadvantage from achieving their full potential in life).

These are the overriding principles which guide any curriculum development or intervention approach. These principles place the child as an individual at the centre of the educational process and promote a 'Team around the child' approach.

Every Child Matters paved the way for a fundamental shift in the way services for children were delivered. For the first time, the many separate agencies in Education and Social Care combined as Children's Services and closer links were established with Heath Authorities through Children's Trusts.

Building on the foundations of Every Child Matters the National Service Framework for children, young people and maternity services was introduced. One aspect of this was the autism exemplar, following one child's journey from early childhood to adulthood, demonstrating optimal practice.

An earlier, though highly relevant publication making recommendations for the pupil with autism and multi-agency co-operation, was the Good Practice Guidance.

Good Practice Guidance (DfES 2002)

In 2002 the DfES and Department of Health (DOH) produced a set of materials to provide guidance for local authorities working in collaboration with local Health Authorities on meeting the needs of children on the autistic spectrum.

The guidance contained in these two booklets, obtainable free from the DCFS, was drawn up over a period of two years by a working group of professionals experienced in Autism Spectrum Disorders and including representatives from the (then) DfES and the Department of Health. It set out to 'give practical help' to those who make provision for children on the autistic spectrum.

Thus it provides:

- pointers or questions to consider different aspects of provision;
- evidence and features illustrating the extent to which a pointer has been addressed;
- case studies of good practice with illustrations from schools, services, authorities and regions across the UK;
- a self-monitoring tool to enable evaluation and reflection on practice.

The focus is on educational provision and practitioners but multi-agency collaboration and partnership are addressed as essential factors.

The guidance is in two main parts: Guidance on Autistic Spectrum Disorders and Pointers to Good Practice.

In the first part, current understanding of the autistic spectrum and a range of educational interventions, together with a series of key principles are identified and these are intended to underpin all aspects of practice. They are:

- Knowledge and Understanding of Autism:
  - core deficits/differences;
  - psychological underpinnings: the 'social sense deficit' and 'mind-blindness';
  - unique learning style;
  - staff flexibility and resourcefulness.
- Early Identification and Intervention;
- Policy and Planning – at daily/local and regional/strategic levels;
- Family Support and Partnership:
  - stress placed on family by child on the autistic spectrum;
  - support for parental knowledge and skills.
- Involvement of Children;

- Co-operation with other Agencies;
  - forward planning – pre-empting difficulties;
  - problem-solving and collaboration;
  - transitions between phases.
- Clear Short and Long-term Educational Goals:
  - social – not purely academic;
  - focusing on communication;
  - addressing play, life and leisure skills;
  - facilitating curriculum access;
  - planned management of behaviour.
- Monitoring, Evaluation and Research to enhance practice and share findings.

In the second part, the set of pointers for good practice cover:

- Advocacy;
- Early Years;
- Family support and short breaks;
- Funding;
- Home-based provision;
- Identification;
- Information and communication technology;
- In-service training;
- LEA Outreach Support Services;
- LEA Policy;
- Mainstream or special school placement decisions;
- Multi-agency support;
- Regional co-ordination;
- School provision for children on the autistic spectrum;
- Speech and Language Therapy;
- Transitions and Moving to Post-School Provision.

It is suggested that providers might want to rate their services against each pointer, using the guidance as a self-evaluation tool. For many of the pointers, examples of good practice are given on the website www.dfes.gov.uk/sen.

One factor within this guidance is to suggest ways of helping teachers and practitioners remove barriers to curriculum access for pupils on the autistic spectrum. The secondary curriculum amendments should facilitate further flexibility towards this end.

National Curriculum amendments (2008)

Primary (Key Stages 1 and 2)

It should be noted that the most fundamental review of the primary curriculum for a decade is currently underway. The aim is to create a new primary curriculum that will raise standards further and help schools achieve the ambitions of the Children's Plan and the outcomes of Every Child Matters. The new curriculum is due to be in place in 2011. At the time of writing, the particular implications for children on the autistic spectrum are not known.

Secondary (Key Stage 3)

A major review of the secondary curriculum in England has seen the 'one size fits all' curriculum replaced by a curriculum that offers more flexibility to tailor teaching to pupils' needs and aspirations. There is now more emphasis on developing in-depth understanding of the key ideas and practice of particular subjects (i.e. English, Maths and ICT) while retaining core elements of the National Curriculum.

Teachers have more power to help children master the basics as well as greater flexibility to find ways of teaching that engage pupils and motivate them to improve their access to learning and stretch pupils who are high fliers. It is also envisaged that the emphasis on using the curriculum as a whole to develop general skills such as initiative, enterprise and the capacity to learn independently will better prepare pupils for GCSEs, the new diplomas and life after school.

One of the major changes is around the personalisation of learning. It is up to individual schools to decide how to teach the curriculum, and there is the flexibility to personalise learning and design a curriculum that meets the needs of their learners. This should help during transition and for those pupils who do not learn in a conventional way as it will be possible for individual needs to be taken into account when designing the curriculum.

'Personalisation' is the new catchphrase. It is one that should appeal to those who work with young people with Asperger syndrome as personalisation is the process of making what is taught and learnt, and how it is taught and learnt, match as closely as possible to the needs of the learner – in other words, making reasonable adjustments for the learning style(s) of the young person with Asperger syndrome based on those described in the following chapter. For teachers it means observing learners closely, recognising their strengths and areas for further development and drawing on the full repertoire of skills and strategies to meet their needs. For learners it means being engaged not just with the content of what is being taught, but being involved with the learning process, understanding what they need to do to improve and taking responsibility for furthering their own progress. For school leaders it means constantly thinking about routines and the organisation of learning for all pupils so that their welfare and their progress can be mutually supportive. In a similar way, assessment can be personalised to ensure that it supports learning and enables all students to demonstrate the progress they have achieved.

The changes to the Key Stage 3 curriculum were to be phased in over a three-year period. It became statutory for Year 7 pupils in September 2008 and for Year 8 pupils in September 2009. It will become statutory for Year 9 in September 2010.

Secondary (Key Stage 4)

In September 2003 it was announced that the curriculum for Key Stage 4 was to change. The main aims seek to offer greater flexibility and choice for students. Building on from the Key Stage 3 curriculum, it is no longer acceptable that all students follow the same journey through the curriculum (which resulted in students leaving school without any qualifications to introduce them to the world of work).

All students have to learn English, maths, science, ICT and PE with an emphasis on health and fitness. It will also be necessary for work-related learning to be delivered. Students will also study citizenship, religious education, sex education and careers education.

It is expected that individual schools will offer a specialist area of study (e.g. engineering). It is expected that students from other schools who want a career in that specialist area will attend the 'specialist' school to study that subject. A new qualification is being introduced; it will be known as a diploma. The diploma will provide students with an integrated programme of study made up of different courses and awards. Foundation and Higher Diploma students can go on to study for the next level of diploma, take a different type of qualification (e.g. GCSE, A level or apprenticeship) or go on to a job with training. An advanced diploma can lead on to university or into a career. The diploma will help students make decisions about their future direction without closing down options. Diploma students will also acquire the skills and knowledge, which are essential for success in employment and higher education, both related to the discipline and those which are common, like teamwork, self-management and critical thinking skills.

For the young person with Asperger syndrome, the vision underpinning the 14–19 reforms is just what is needed: offering young people the subjects that motivate them, in a style and at a time that suits them, so that all young people will want to stay beyond the age of 16 and be enabled to acquire essential skills for living.

Inclusion Development Programme (IDP) (2009)

The Inclusion Development Programme (IDP) was initiated to increase the confidence and expertise of mainstream practitioners in promoting curriculum access for pupils with SEN in mainstream settings and schools. In 2008, the DCSF instigated a four-year IDP, under the National Strategies umbrella, with the aim of supporting schools and early years settings in their work with children with additional needs through web-based and DVD materials, including:

- teaching and learning resources;
- training materials;
- guidance on effective classroom strategies;
- models of good practice for multi-disciplinary teams;
- information about sources of more specialist advice.

Specific sets of materials were designed to support practitioners working with children on the autistic spectrum. These were produced by National Strategies in conjunction with the Autism Centre for Education and Research at the University of Birmingham. The two autism-specific resources, launched in March 2009, are:

- *Supporting children on the autism spectrum*, which is for early years settings (e.g. childminders, playgroups, nurseries and children's centres);

- *Supporting pupils on the autism spectrum*, which is designed for headteachers, Special Educational Needs Coordinators (SENCOs), leadership teams, governors, teachers, teaching assistants and all students training to be teachers, and for all mainstream primary and secondary schools.

Both resources are also useful for parents and carers. In addition, they are helpful to professionals in a number of agencies in raising awareness of the needs of children and young people on the autism spectrum. They can be accessed at www.standards.dcsf.gov.uk/nationalstrategies.

Disability Discrimination Act (1995)

Further aspects of the educational framework stem from the Disability Discrimination Act (DDA) (1995). To support schools and local authorities in implementing their duties under the DDA, the government drew together the Disability Equality Duty. In 2006 the government decided to link together the important legislation surrounding the lives of children and young people with disabilities in the Disability Equality Duty. The Duty does not bring in new rights for children and young people with disabilities, but it does require schools to take a more proactive approach to promoting disability equality and eliminating discrimination.

The Disability Discrimination Act 1995 (DDA) defines a disabled person as someone who has 'a physical or mental impairment which has a substantial and long-term adverse effect on his or her ability to carry out normal day-to-day activities'. This DDA definition is broad and includes a wide range of impairments including learning disabilities, Autistic Spectrum Disorders, dyslexia, diabetes and epilepsy where the effect of the impairment on the pupil's ability to carry out normal day-to-day activity is adverse, substantial and long term.

The DDA requires schools to:

- not to treat pupils with disabilities 'less favourably';

- make reasonable adjustments to ensure that pupils with disabilities are not at a substantial disadvantage;

- draw up school accessibility plans to show how, over time, they will increase access to education for pupils with disabilities by increasing access to the curriculum, making improvements to the physical environment of the school to increase access and making written information accessible to pupils in a range of different ways;

- comply with the Disability Equality Duty;

- prepare, publish, implement and report on a Disability Equality Scheme.

The Disability Equality Duty includes an important duty to eliminate harassment of disabled children and young people that is related to their disability. Schools therefore need to tackle the bullying of children with SEN and disabilities as part of complying with this part of the Disability Equality Duty. (See section on Asperger syndrome and bullying.)

As mentioned, under the DDA, schools are expected to make reasonable adjustments for pupils with disabilities and draw up school accessibility plans.

Making reasonable adjustments for pupils on the autism spectrum

Reasonable adjustments aim to ensure that the pupil's disability is not a barrier to accessing the world of school. When deciding if a reasonable adjustment is necessary, schools need to consider the potential impact on pupils with disabilities in terms of:

- time and effort;
- inconvenience;
- indignity or discomfort;
- loss of opportunity;
- progress.

Schools should be making reasonable adjustments at different levels of school life:

- for the individual;
- in their practices and procedures;
- in their policies.

Alfie expressed his own views about reasonable adjustments. Alfie is a very articulate Year 6 pupil with Asperger syndrome. At the end of a frustrating week he approached his teacher and asked, 'Which part of my disability did you consider in your planning this week?'

To make reasonable adjustments schools will need to:

- plan ahead;
- identify potential barriers;
- work collaboratively with pupils with disabilities, their parents and others;
- identify practical solutions through a problem-solving approach;
- ensure that staff have the necessary skills;
- monitor the effects of adjustments on a pupil's progress.

Schools are more likely to succeed in their efforts to make reasonable adjustments when everyone who works in the school and the governors are involved. Schools will know they are succeeding when:

- pupils with disabilities feel part of the life of the school;
- pupils with disabilities are included by their peers in all parts of school life;
- parents feel their disabled child is part of the life of the school;
- staff feel confident working with pupils with disabilities.

Case study

When Malcolm was in Year 10 he was expected to undertake a work experience placement. His parents wanted this placement to be within the 'safe' environment of the school library. On the surface, this appeared to be a reasonable adjustment. However, it would have been a lost opportunity to prepare Malcolm for life after school. So together with parents and school staff, the specialist advisory teacher identified the main issues. They were:

- safety awareness (as Malcolm would wander off and get lost);
- independent travel skills (as Malcolm had never been anywhere without his family);
- concern that the staff in the workplace would not understand Malcolm's difficulties;
- concern that Malcolm would not be able to cope with the variety of tasks asked of him.

The teacher undertook a travel training programme and an orientation programme based on the independence and mobility work undertaken with pupils with a visual impairment. The placement was carefully vetted, staff were given information to aid understanding and the teacher contacted the key member of staff regularly.

It was a very successful placement that helped Malcolm to understand what the concept of work was that was referred to so often. Malcolm and his mum still update the key staff member on his progress. The staff in the placement felt they benefited from having Malcolm with them and have offered to take any of the pupils on the autism spectrum in the future.

School accessibility plans

The accessibility plan has an important part to play in improving outcomes for pupils with disabilities and raising standards in schools. To be effective it has to: be grounded in the ethos of good practice for all; include pupils' and parents' views in the planning process; use hard and soft data on inclusion; and be part of the school improvement programme. There are statutory requirements that must be taken into account when compiling the plan. The plan must:

- be in writing;
- cover the three strands of increasing access over time: increased access to the curriculum; improvements to the physical environment; and improvements in the provision of information for pupils with disabilities;
- be adequately resourced, implemented, reviewed and revised as necessary;
- be renewed every three years;
- be reported to parents annually.

The Autism Education Trust (AET) (established 2007)

The Autism Education Trust (AET) is a national body which was launched in November 2007 with funding from the DCSF. It is dedicated to coordinating and improving education support for all children on the autism spectrum in England.

The AET brings together a cross-section of people with experience of the autism spectrum. The AET aims to:

- raise awareness of the importance of appropriate educational provision for children and young people on the autism spectrum;
- bring organisations involved in delivering autism education services together in order to promote good practice and share information;
- involve children and young people on the autism spectrum (together with their families and carers) in the planning and delivery of information and resources to enhance and improve autism education across the country;
- commission research in order to remain relevant and fully informed of current practice across England;
- provide a platform for the promotion and sharing of good practice that succeeds in improving the education needs of children and young people on the autism spectrum;
- provide a link between users, professionals, policy makers and central government involved with autism education.

The AET website, which contains a wealth of resources, can be accessed at www. autismeducationtrust.org.uk.

Summary

The legislation and guidance described in this chapter emphasise the importance of the following factors:

- an holistic view of the child;
- planning centred on the child;
- multi-agency collaboration;
- school self-evaluation;
- increased flexibility within the curriculum;
- willingness to make reasonable adjustments.

All this needs to be underpinned by a thorough awareness of the autism spectrum and the child's individual presentation.

Educational intervention in practice

Hans Asperger felt that educational 'training' would help the child, and for the majority of children this has proved to be the case. To be effective, intervention for children with Asperger syndrome must be grounded in an understanding of the nature of the condition and its fundamental impairments.

Allowance needs to be made for individuality as no two children are affected in exactly the same way.

Networks of support

Many local authorities have developed an authority-wide network of support designed to meet the needs of children with autism and Asperger syndrome. These networks are usually based on the following elements:

- a shared understanding of autism and Asperger syndrome;
- educational provision preceded by quality assessment;
- authority-wide availability of specialist advice;
- careful selection and training of support teachers and assistants;
- professional links between specialist schools and mainstream schools and between professionals from different agencies.

Although intervention may appear to be specialist, it does not necessarily mean that the child with Asperger syndrome has to attend a specialist school. It is possible to take the specialism to the child and enrich the mainstream situation so that, through understanding and differentiation, the child is part of the community of the school and is valued as an individual within this community. Key roles in an ideal support network are those of the SENCO, the class teacher, the support teacher and the support assistant.

The role of the Special Educational Needs Coordinator (SENCO)

The role of the SENCO is important in ensuring collaboration between external agencies, the family and the school in meeting the needs of a pupil with Asperger syndrome and in further ensuring that:

- the pupil's records include information from assessment, including suggested intervention strategies, and that this information informs planning including IEPs and school accessibility plans;

- this information is shared with teaching and support staff within the school and also with the parents;
- parents are given the opportunity to meet the SENCO and class teacher on a regular basis;
- the pupils' reviews are person-centred, ensuring that their views are taken into account;
- support is enlisted from support services, health and social services and voluntary agencies as appropriate;
- training for staff is made available as appropriate;
- a resource bank is maintained;
- the pupil's progress is carefully monitored and reviewed.

The role of the class teacher

The role of the class teacher is central to the education of the child with Asperger syndrome. The role can be likened to that of an orchestral conductor, pivotal in keeping everything together and in tune. It is their job to ensure that all children in the class are educated at a level appropriate to their needs. To do this, it is necessary to create an environment that encourages valuing of individuals and recognises different learning styles. This is based on having an understanding of the needs of all the children, including the child with Asperger syndrome.

Particular areas on which the class teacher will focus are:

- creating a calm working environment;
- ensuring that the structure of the classroom is clearly laid out;
- modifying tasks to harness and build on the child's strengths;
- making sure that the child understands what is expected of him;
- introducing choice gradually, encouraging decision making;
- grading tasks, gradually increasing demands on the child;
- directing the child's attention at an individual level, rather than relying on whole class instructions;
- accessing available training;
- planning IEPs;
- recording and monitoring progress;
- evaluating intervention strategies;
- working closely with the available support network;
- establishing and maintaining home–school links.

While this may at first appear to be a challenging set of expectations, it is really just an example of good classroom practice.

An important thought to keep in mind is that the child with Asperger syndrome is part of the whole school community and should be accepted and supported by the whole school community.

The role of the support teacher

The support teacher is well placed to bring specialist understanding of Asperger syndrome into the mainstream classroom. A large part of the role is to increase the confidence of all those involved in the education of the child with Asperger syndrome. This includes boosting the confidence of the child himself and that of his parents. If all concerned feel positive, then the priority, particularly if any difficulties are met, will be to move forward and find solutions.

The effective support teacher will have:

- a thorough understanding of Asperger syndrome and its educational implications;
- experience working with children with Asperger syndrome across a range of settings;
- the ability to see the world from the child's point of view, and to interpret that view for others;
- the sensitivity to understand the class teacher's perspective and the factors which may constrain her;
- skills in assessing the child in his particular context;
- the ability to advise on ways of manipulating the classroom environment so that it suits the child's learning style;
- an open-minded, positive attitude and the ability to remain calm;
- skills in delivering in-service training (INSET);
- knowledge of ways in which the curriculum may effectively be differentiated;
- the ability to foster good relationships with parents, school staff and other professionals, recognising the need for reassurance.

The support teacher may not have all the answers, but will be able to suggest a range of strategies and approaches for the class teacher and support assistant to employ. The development of an atmosphere of mutual trust will be a priority.

The role of the support assistant

The classroom support assistant has a role in relation to the child with Asperger syndrome which differs from the approach to a child with learning difficulties. Very often, children with Asperger syndrome are more comfortable when carrying out learning tasks than when playing. The routine and clear structure of a learning task can be easier to cope with, as long as social interaction with other children is not essential.

Because of the subtle and pervasive nature of the impairment, it is in the ordinariness of moment-by-moment existence that difficulties may occur for the child with Asperger syndrome. The support assistant, therefore, has to be prepared to operate at an equally subtle and pervasive level, be present in the fabric of the child's day, be part of the prosthetic environment and act as translator, go-between and friend.

Working in close cooperation with the class teacher, school SENCO, specialist support teacher (where available), other involved professionals and parents, the support assistant has to, where possible:

- understand the child's limited ability to interpret social cues;
- interpret situations for the child;

- show the child what is expected of him;
- help in the teaching of appropriate social interaction skills (e.g. taking turns);
- guide peers in how to interact with the pupil and engage their help;
- understand the subtle difficulties of language and communication;
- listen to the child's pattern of language use and be alert to difficulties of interpretation;
- explain, show and make clear to the child when confusion occurs;
- help the child to develop appropriate language use and awareness;
- understand the sources of rigidity and obsessiveness in the child's behaviour;
- anticipate what will cause anxiety, and make changes accordingly;
- analyse and break down situations or activities which cause alarm;
- make task procedures clearly visible with visual and pictorial cues;
- support the child in physical activities if clumsiness is a problem;
- assist in making writing tasks easier;
- be prepared for periods of anxiety with appropriate stress-reducing activities;
- evaluate the potential for increasing the child's independence on a regular basis;
- identify gaps in the development of self-help skills (in areas such as dressing and washing), and incorporate these skills into the child's programme;
- identify any organisation difficulties and produce practical and visual aids to help the child;
- support home–school liaison and the recording of progress;
- offer appropriate rewarding strategies within individual programmes;
- know when and how to ask for help from teaching and specialist support staff;
- liaise regularly with the class teacher, school SENCO and specialist teaching support staff (if available);
- develop and maintain useful monitoring, evaluating and recording systems.

In addition, the support assistant will need to be calm, positive and consistent, and will preferably have a good sense of humour!

Top tips for support assistants

The following is a list of ideas compiled by a group of some 30 support assistants attending a workshop on autism and Asperger syndrome. They were each asked to recommend five 'top tips' derived from their experience of working with children with Asperger syndrome.

COMMUNICATION

- Simplify your language.
- Give one instruction at a time, not a sequence.
- Keep facial expressions and gestures simple and clear.
- Give the child time to respond.

- Use additional visual clues to help the child understand.
- Be sensitive to the child's attempts to communicate.
- Set up situations which will encourage the child to attempt to communicate.

SOCIAL INTERACTION

- Understand that the child may feel threatened by the close proximity of others, especially those his own age.
- Allow for solitariness.
- Go at the child's pace when trying to develop interaction. (You may need to 'move down' developmentally.)
- Identify what the child likes and dislikes socially, and use this knowledge when planning activities.
- The child is more likely to interact with familiar people, so give him time to get to know you and don't confuse him with many changes of personnel.

BEHAVIOUR

- Offer maximum consistency of approach.
- Help the child understand what is expected of him by having clear, predictable routines.
- Introduce any changes gradually.
- Help explain changes by giving visual clues.
- If the child becomes agitated, understand that the usual strategies for calming a child (e.g., trying to sit him on your knee) may have the opposite effect, winding him up even more.
- If the child has an obsession, don't try to stop it. In time, you may be able to limit it; in the meantime use it positively.

GENERAL

- Results and progress can be slow, but don't give up! (It often takes a long time to form a relationship.)
- Every child is different; what works for one may not work for another.
- Every child is variable; if the child is having a bad day, don't feel that it is your fault.
- If all else fails, leave alone. Tomorrow is another day!

Because the long-term aim is for the child with Asperger syndrome to function independently, the best support assistant is the one who does herself out of a job!

Key elements of effective intervention

The key words for intervention are: routine, clarity and consistency. Minor environmental changes in the classroom, which simplify the organisation and structure of the room and the tasks, can help the child make sense of expectations.

Useful changes can be made in the following areas:

- the physical and sensory environment;
- the language and communication environment;
- the social environment;
- the curricular environment.

Specific interventions to enable the child to develop skills and understanding in the areas of social interaction, social communication and social imagination and play can then be built in. In other words, the approach needs to be remedial as well as compensatory.

The physical and sensory environment

A cluttered, unpredictable, ever-changing environment will only confuse the child with Asperger syndrome and make him anxious. By analysing the child's learning environment, it is possible to devise modifications which will help him.

Organisation and structure

Most classrooms are organised along social lines. The role of social understanding is taken for granted by teachers who may, in fact, not be aware of the role of social understanding within the organisation of their classroom (e.g. in collaborative group work, the sharing of equipment and listening as a group to an instruction). A lot of infant and primary classrooms are organised on group lines, with groups moving around the classroom to access tasks.

It may be necessary to give the child his own space at times during the day. This will be particularly important when a new task is being introduced, since the stress of being part of a group may limit understanding. This space does not need to be a sophisticated individual workstation; a desk placed adjacent to the group table, facing away from distractions, can be effective.

It is helpful if the child has a designated seating position within the classroom and keeps the same tray or drawer throughout the year. Where changes need to be made, they must be explained simply and carefully in advance.

Most children happily adapt to the structure of the classroom and are able to make sense of what is happening. However, the child with Asperger syndrome may need an extra layer of structure to help him access the curriculum.

Supertactic: Treatment and Education of Autistic and Communication-Handicapped Children (TEACCH)

This extra layer of structure is a visual layer. The foundation for this approach can be found within a system developed in North Carolina called Treatment and Education of Autistic and Communication-Handicapped Children (TEACCH). The TEACCH system (Schopler *et al.* 1995) recognises that, for children with autism spectrum disorders, the total psychological environment is an important avenue of intervention.

TEACCH was developed in the 1960s by Eric Schopler and Gary Mesibov for use with children with autism. Seen as a 'cradle to grave' approach, it starts with a

---

comprehensive assessment, progresses through structured intervention and aims to equip students for productive life in the community.

Whereas the TEACCH environment for children with autism is described as 'prosthetic', in respect of Asperger syndrome its use may be better described as 'scaffolding'. In the latter case, the degree of environmental modification will be steadily modified over time, rather than being maintained as long-term provision. The main elements of TEACCH are as follows.

PHYSICAL STRUCTURE

This refers to the way in which the environment is organised. There are clear visual boundaries segmenting the space into recognisable parts, which help the children understand what they are expected to do in each area. In the area set aside for work, distractions are kept to a minimum.

THE SCHEDULE

This visually tells the child what activities will occur, and in which order. Using objects, photos, pictures, numbers or words (depending on the individual's developmental level), the child is helped to understand a sequence of events.

Figure 5.1 Picture schedule

WORK SYSTEMS

Through these systems the child is taught:

- How much work will I have to do?
- What work will I have to do?
- When will I have finished?
- What happens when I've finished?

VISUAL CLARITY

Tasks are presented visually so as to make the expectations clear and highlight the important information.

   The following case study is an example of this style of intervention.

- Dean, an eight-year-old boy, was diagnosed at the age of four as having Asperger syndrome. His school career began in an assessment class of 12 pupils attached to a mainstream infant school.
- Dean found the situation very difficult. He would scream and become upset at any changes that took place within the school day.
- Photographs were taken of all the activities likely to be on offer in the class.
- A series of these photographs was stuck on the wall, in the order that activities would happen that day, by Dean's table.
- Staff drew Dean's attention to the first photograph, introducing him to his first task.
- On completion of this task, Dean would remove this photo and see what was to be done next. In this way, Dean began to be able to predict what was to happen next. This enabled him to relax within the situation and access the curriculum.
- Once Dean was at ease with the photograph timetable, it was replaced by a series of line drawings and words.
- From this, the drawings were replaced with words alone, which, in turn, became a daily list. Dean crossed off each activity as it was completed.
- At this time it was thought that Dean was ready to move into the mainstream infant class on a full-time basis.
- At his review, prior to the move, it was agreed that his Statement should be amended to include help from a Special Support Assistant (SSA) as he moved on.
- The structure continued in the mainstream classroom (a Year 1 class of 28 children with one teacher). Dean's SSA prepared the list each morning and Dean used it as a way of supporting his understanding of what was happening.
- The list began to be condensed to cover just the main points of the day.
- The list eventually became redundant, without repercussions.

- When Dean moved up to the junior school, his timetable was briefly reintroduced, until he had settled, then phased out again.

The visual support offered to Dean appeared to enable him to engage with the activities by giving an extra layer of structure and predictability in his classroom. Other children have adopted personal ways of structuring tasks to help their understanding. One five-year-old boy would use his fingers to list the order of classroom activities. Some others have used a series of comic strip style drawings to guide them through the day. It helps motivate the child if a reward activity is included in the sequence.

Mesibov and Howley (2003) give a detailed account of the many ways in which visual structure can be used to support learning and social development.

The language and communication environment

Children with Asperger syndrome often have good language skills, including extensive vocabularies and the ability to use complex grammatical structures. However, these skills are superficial and mask their difficulties in communication – particularly in the social use of language (pragmatics) and the ability to convey and understand meaning (semantics). These children do not learn the necessary pragmatic and semantic skills from simply being surrounded by a communication-rich environment.

The aim of intervention is to create an environment which will:

- help the child to develop both verbal and non-verbal communicative intent;
- develop the child's ability to initiate and maintain a conversation;
- enhance the child's understanding of meaning.

Intervention should start at the child's communication level rather than the language level. Although his communication skills may not be developing along the usual lines, he is making a real attempt to enter the communicative process. Our responses to him should reflect this.

Structuring the language environment

It helps if the language environment can be simplified, structured and take account of the following points:

- Address the child by name before giving an instruction, particularly if instructing the class as a group.
- Encourage and reinforce all attempts to communicate.
- Use concrete, direct and explicit instructions which are supported by picture prompts where possible.
- If you need to give a sequence of instructions, give just one step at a time.
- Give the child time to respond to an instruction, then check that he has understood.
- If necessary, repeat an instruction without rewording it (or the child may think it is a different instruction).

- Teach the child a stock phrase to use when he does not understand an instruction – this may prevent frustration on both sides.

- Questions often confuse children with Asperger syndrome. Where possible, turn them into statements. (For example, 'The weather today is …' rather than 'What's the weather like today?')

- Recognise the child's intentions. (For example, they may say, 'Do you want some crisps?' but mean '*I* want some crisps'.)

- Guide the child towards the correct response for different situations.

- When looking at text or listening to people speak, draw the child's attention to the way words are usually put together.

- Try to be aware of the language you use and consider whether or not it could be misinterpreted. Take care not to use sarcasm or irony.

- Offer activities which present opportunities for turn-taking and reciprocity.

Developing the child's skills and understanding

- A key role is that of interpreter, someone who can help the child to make sense of the world and help the world understand the child. This may be a support assistant, but classmates can also have a role here.

- If the child echoes words or chunks of language (echolalia), it could mean that he has failed to understand. It may also be an indication of anxiety. Simplify your language and check for stress triggers.

- If the child has particular areas of skill or interest, use these as starting points for language work.

- Help the child to become aware of the needs of the listener, learning how to vary the tone and volume of his voice according to the situation.

- Encourage eye-to-eye contact without training it.

- The child may understand literal rather than metaphorical or implied meanings. Go through some common metaphors with him (e.g. 'Pull your socks up!') and explain what they mean. Spell out your implied meanings. (For example, you may say, 'It's very noisy in here' but you mean 'Be quiet everyone.'.) Elizabeth Newson (1992) advises that deliberately teaching a repertoire of metaphors can be productive, and suggests the use of a series of children's booklets by Len Collis, called 'Things We Say: A Book that Helps You Understand What People Mean'. She also indicates the importance of cultivating a verbal sense of humour, using children's illustrated joke books as a starting point and graduating to comic strip books such as *Fungus the Bogeyman*, to encourage an appreciation of irony and satire.

- Help the child to understand the meaning and emotions behind certain facial expressions. Draw his attention to pictures in books and magazines which illustrate different expressions, and to his own face in the mirror. Role-play can be useful for some children in acting out situations involving emotional reactions. Video feedback can help the child to recognise emotions expressed in facial expression, posture and gesture.

- The Social Use of Language Programme (SULP) (Rinaldi 1992) provides an assessment tool, together with intervention programmes designed to develop social and pragmatic language understanding and use. For most children, language is a way of entering a stimulating social world. This is not necessarily the case for children with Asperger syndrome.

The social environment

The difficulty in developing fluent interpersonal skills is probably the most noticeable feature of children with Asperger syndrome. These children are not antisocial. Rather, they are asocial, at times wanting to be part of the social world, but not knowing how to enter it. But children with Asperger syndrome do not pick up social skills incidentally; they need to be specifically taught.

Intervention must start at the child's level of interaction, recognising that he is socially immature, whatever his level of academic performance. It must be borne in mind that the child may be content in solitary pursuits. One should not force the child to join in, but take the approach of enhancing his social skills. The classroom environment should take account of the anxiety that a child can feel by being part of a group. There should be opportunities for the child to have his own space at times.

Other people need to understand the difficulties posed by the child with Asperger syndrome and the reasons why he behaves the way he does. These children appear to find it easier to relate to adults than to others their own age. This may be because adults make more allowances and modify their own behaviour towards the child.

The child with Asperger syndrome may appear to be naive and trusting, unable to discriminate between friendly approaches and those approaches which are intended to wind them up. Their peers seem to take on the role of buddy or bully.

Intervention starts with observation, identifying which children act positively and which children are potential sources of anxiety. This anxiety may not be immediately obvious. The child with Asperger syndrome may brood on his perception of an incident, reacting negatively at a later date.

Consider the following points when planning intervention:

- Ensure that all staff have an awareness of the social difficulties arising from Asperger syndrome, and are prepared to make allowances in an agreed way.

- With parental agreement, it may be helpful to talk to others in the class or school about Asperger syndrome.

- As part of a general school policy of positive behaviour management, ensure that all children are aware of the unacceptability of bullying.

- Teach the child how to respond to unwanted approaches since a child who is tormented may become increasingly hostile and aggressive.

- Make sure the child knows which adult to turn to when feeling upset.

- Consider having a quiet area available for the child to retreat to when feeling anxious.

- Analyse the class group and select mature children to act as buddies or a 'Circle of Friends'.

The buddy system involves identifying another child who is willing to help the child with Asperger syndrome to negotiate difficulties. When Philip was encouraged to leave the gatepost and come into school, he was given the support of a buddy. This boy helped Philip to get organised for lessons, follow his timetable and be in the right place at the right time. In return, Philip drew on his own skills to help him with work on the computer. Circles of Friends can be built up so that the onus does not fall only on one child.

Supertactic: Circle of Friends

Circle of Friends is a strategy originally developed in Canada in order to promote the inclusion of pupils with various special educational needs in mainstream settings. It focuses on enlisting fellow pupils to support the target child. The approach has been implemented in the UK and has been shown to be particularly helpful in supporting inclusion of pupils within the autism spectrum (Whitaker *et al.* 1998).

A Circle of Friends is usually made up of 6–8 pupils from the child's class group who meet on a weekly basis with the focus child and an adult leading the group.

The aim of the Circle of Friends is to acknowledge and focus on the pupil's strengths and progress and to identify difficulties in a supportive way. Targets and strategies are then identified by the group to help and support the focus child to tackle difficulties. The group then puts their ideas into practice and comes back to review in following meetings.

Before initiating a Circle of Friends, the permission of the child concerned and the family should be sought. Guidelines are offered to staff who wish to use this approach by Newton and Wilson (1999) and an example of how this approach has been used with children with autism has been detailed by Whitaker *et al.* (1998).

Additional resources within children's literature

With greater understanding and awareness of the autism spectrum has come an increasing interest from children's authors, who include child characters in their stories and often sensitively convey some of the issues involved. For younger children, *Looking after Louis* by Lesley Ely captures the rhythm and tone of the young autistic child's echolalic speech and the initial bewilderment and eventual support of classmates. It is beautifully illustrated by Polly Dunbar. *My Brother Sammy* by Becky Edwards and David Armitage treats the subject from the point of view of a sibling. It has vivid colour-wash illustrations. It is also an excellent resource for Key Stage 1 and Key Stage 2 class groups. For secondary Key Stage 3 and some Key Stage 2 readers, Julia Jarman's *Hangman* treats the subject of bullying with an 'undisclosed' Asperger syndrome young boy as its main character in a fast-paced story set on a school trip to France. (A scheme of work for use with Year 7 classes is available on her website: www.juliajarman.com.) All of these books are supportive of inclusion, hoping to develop peer awareness of children on the autism spectrum in mainstream settings and developing awareness through metaphor and story and appealing to the imagination and powers of empathy of the peer group!

Developing the child's skills and understanding

THE SENSE OF SELF

It is often said that children with Asperger syndrome have a high level of egocentricity. This may make it sound as if they choose to act in this way – they don't! They often don't even understand their own feelings and behaviour. There may come a time when the child is concerned as to his own well-being. Questions in adolescence from able children, such as 'Am I mad?', cause distress to all concerned. The aim of intervention is to increase the child's confidence in himself as an individual, since increased self-esteem reduces anxiety. The following points should be borne in mind:

- There is a need to strive to give the child a positive self-image.
- The time will come when it will be appropriate to tell the child the background to his difficulties. How and when to do this will need to be discussed by parents and professionals. The following resources are likely to be helpful: Mesibov and Faherty (2000); Gray (1994a); and Vermeulen (2001).
- Once the child is aware of his diagnosis, discourage him from blaming Asperger syndrome for everything. Encourage him to think of alternative strategies.
- The child may need to be taught to develop a sense of self. Encourage him to reflect on his own role in events and activities, using photographs or video and subjective accounts. Jordan and Powell (1995) explain how this approach is developed.

INTERACTION WITH OTHERS

Children with Asperger syndrome lack an awareness of the needs of others in relation to themselves. Intervention aims to increase the child's desire to interact with others. It may start with increasing the child's awareness of the ways in which other people behave, then work to equip the child to interact with others. To do this it is necessary to teach specific social skills, preferably in realistic, functional settings:

- Identify areas of social interaction where the child particularly struggles (e.g. how to enter a group, how to talk about things that interest others – not simply pet interests and how to stay involved in the group topic). Analyse the skills he needs to improve his performance and teach them in small, achievable steps.
- Make the most of activities which lend themselves to working with a partner (e.g. paired reading).
- Give the child the opportunity to play simple board games (e.g., draughts) with a partner. Initially the partner may be a trusted adult, later introducing another child to the game.
- Begin to involve the child in simple team games in the classroom, PE or the playground. Make the child's role in the game very clear.

'Social Stories' (Carol Gray 1994b) are particularly effective in enabling children to understand specific social situations which may cause difficulty.

Supertactic: Social Stories

Social Stories (Gray 1994b) were originally devised by Carol Gray in response to a sudden insight she had while attempting to change the behaviour of a student who continually called out across an auditorium full of peers to the lecturer addressing them. Despite her extensive experience of working with youngsters on the autism spectrum, her tried and tested strategies failed. Carol realised in discussion with the student that he simply believed that the lecturer was addressing him directly. He was oblivious to the true nature of the situation; he lacked the required social understanding which would enable him to behave appropriately.

The emphasis, therefore, in developing Social Stories to use with children and young people on the autism spectrum is not to change behaviour by obtaining compliance, but to share accurate information and understanding about a situation – specifically to give detailed information about what the individual might expect from the situation and what might be expected from him.

Social Stories then, are written as relatively short, straightforward descriptions of social situations to inform and advise the individual about a particular situation which may be troubling him or to help prepare for social events. Gray (1994b) recommends that at least 50 per cent of all Social Stories developed for a specific child, adolescent or adult on the autism spectrum must applaud what that person currently does well. Similarly her stories themselves are to be written in a reassuring and patient style, avoiding a 'corrective tone'.

Key features of Social Stories are that they are:

- **permanent** – the child can read the Social Story over and over again and there is no emphasis on fading the use of the Social Story, rather the opposite so that the necessary social information can be revisited.

- **written in simple language** – language which reflects the pupil's own.

- **based on observations** – before writing, observations are made of the child and discussions are held with other staff, family members, those who know the child best and also with the student himself. Carol Gray stresses that the process of writing the story is as important as the product.

- **explicit** – the social story makes rules, expectations and codes of behaviour explicit where these are often implicit or assumed.

- **factual** – the pupil is offered information about who is doing what and why.

- **focused on thoughts and feelings** – describing what other people are thinking and feeling and how that relates to their behaviour.

- **written in a predictable style**.

Gray (1994b) outlines a specific structure for the social story. The basic social story structure consists of descriptive sentences which are objective, often observable statements of fact that are free of interpretation (e.g. 'There are four people in my family', or 'My mum usually makes my sandwiches in the morning'). These can stand alone as a story. Additionally 'perspective' sentences are usually included. These describe the thoughts and feelings and/or beliefs of other people in the situation (e.g. 'My friend will like it when I give him his birthday present' or 'Children know that when Mrs D turns off the light it is time for morning break'). Finally, the 'directive' sentence tells the child what he or she can or may do in the situation or provides a range of responses for the child in that situation (e.g. 'I will try to stand quietly in the dinner queue and wait my turn' or 'I can close my eyes and count to ten'). There must be at least twice as many descriptive and perspective sentences as directive sentences.

The story may also contain 'affirmative' sentences, which express a common or shared opinion or value (e.g. 'This is a good idea' or 'This is okay'). The story may also contain 'cooperative' sentences, which explain what others will do in support of the child.

The story is written from a first-person perspective as though the child is describing the event (in the case of younger children) or a third-person perspective (like a newspaper article) for an older child or adolescent.

The story follows a basic format of an introduction clearly identifying the topic, a body that adds detail and a conclusion. The title of the story should reflect the focus of the story, emphasising the main point, thus compensating for the deficit in 'central coherence' in the autistic thinking style. Illustrations meaningful to the child may be used to enhance the meaning of the text.

Social Stories have now been successfully used across a wide age-range of children from explaining 'A Hug' and 'Carpet Time' in the early years to 'How to Blow Your Nose', 'How to Line Up in the Dinner Queue', 'Managing Time on the Computer' and 'Coming into the Classroom' at secondary Key Stages 3 and 4.

Carol Gray (1994b, 2002; Gray and Howley 2005) has published detailed guidelines and many examples of Social Stories for those wishing to use this approach.

The curricular environment

The majority of children with Asperger syndrome are educated within mainstream schools. Some teachers feel overwhelmed by the responsibility of teaching such a child within a class group of 30 or more. This is not for any hostile or negative reasons, but stems from anxiety about the unknown. They feel they may have to use strategies that are outside the normal repertoire of teaching in order to meet the child's needs. In reality what is needed is a combination of an understanding of Asperger syndrome and good classroom practice.

Teachers need to be informed, tolerant and empathic. The situation needs to be such that all staff are aware of the educational implications of Asperger syndrome. Specific impairments are part of Asperger syndrome, but each child will have many strengths which can be developed in school.

The Asperger learning style

In Chapter 3, we considered the educational implications of the impairments of Asperger syndrome, and the psychological theories which inform them. It has been suggested that in Asperger syndrome the child's difficulties stem from impairments of Theory of Mind, Central Coherence and Executive Function. Because of this, the child with Asperger syndrome has a different perspective on the world. This perspective is reflected in his learning style. The 'Asperger learning style' is composed of the following characteristics:

- **Motivation.** Competitive motives are absent in the child with Asperger syndrome. He lacks both pride and shame, and he has no desire to stand out.

- **Imitation.** Although he may be able to copy what others do, he finds it hard to adjust these copied movements to his own frame of reference.

- **Perception.** There is a possibility of inconsistent or unexpected responses to sensory input.

- **Attention.** The child's focus of attention is often narrow and/or obsessive. Stimulus characteristics may be combined idiosyncratically.

- **Memory.** The child's memory is likely to be episodic (i.e. events are not stored in the context in which they occurred). Lists of facts may be stored in this way without a meaningful framework to link them.

- **Sequencing.** The child with Asperger syndrome will have difficulty in following sequences. He may be able to match a sequence but be unable to go beyond the model, to abstract the rule or principle on which it is based. For this reason, changes in sequences of events will distress the child because the overarching principle will not have been recognised.

- **Problem solving.** The child tries to learn set responses for set situations. He may learn a set of strategies, but not be aware that he possesses them, and therefore be unable to select an appropriate strategy for a new situation.

Accommodating the Asperger syndrome learning style within the National Curriculum

Running through the National Curriculum are common themes which may need to be differentiated to accommodate the particular learning style of the child with Asperger syndrome. To illustrate this, selected elements of the National Curriculum are viewed from the point of view of a child with Asperger syndrome. Examples of possible difficulty will are outlined, together with suggested intervention strategies.

ENGLISH: KEY STAGES 1 AND 2

In this example, the young child's difficulties in being able to think flexibly and creatively are impeding his progress in English.

Curriculum area: English	Key Stages: 1 and 2
Examples of difficulties	Suggested strategies
1. Child's ability to think imaginatively is impaired, leading to problems in creative writing.	1. Give the child additional opportunities to write about real things he has experienced. Use this as the basis for developing creative writing. 'This is what really happened when you went to the seaside, but what would have happened if it had rained/ the car had broken down/you had lost your spending money?' Help the child by talking through the possibilities. Keep creative elements within the child's experience.
2. The child might be quite skilled at reading. He can decode the words, but doesn't fully understand what he's read.	2. Extend the child's understanding by drawing his attention to the illustrations: 'What's happening in the picture?' Ask him to predict what will happen next: 'What will the boy do now?' Ask him to retell what he's just read. Give preference to books which offer realism rather than fantasy. Give the child ample access to non-fiction books. He will find it easier to retrieve information from these than from stories.

TECHNOLOGY: KEY STAGES 3 AND 4

In this second example, an older student, also limited in his ability to think flexibly, has difficulties with aspects of Technology.

Curriculum area: Technology	Key Stages: 3 and 4
Examples of difficulties	Suggested strategies
1. The student has difficulty with those aspects of Technology which demand a significant level of creative thinking.	1. Choose a project which is practical, relevant to the pupil and can make use of recent direct experience.
2. The student finds it difficult to choose which materials and equipment to use.	2. Don't overwhelm the student with too many items to choose from. Present no more than two alternatives at a time.
3. The student is distracted by irrelevant details. He goes off at a tangent and fails to complete a task.	3. Minimise distractions in the way the materials are set out. Help the student to maintain his focus by offering a written format with the task outlined in clear steps and supported by diagrams.
4. The curriculum expects students to have an open-minded approach when developing their ideas, and to explore a range of potential solutions before selecting one. This student may only see one possibility and stick with it rigidly.	4. At first, go along with his single-mindedness and focus on developing his skills in describing, recording, organising and planning. Later, encourage the consideration of other options and strategies. Structured worksheets may be useful.

MATHS: KEY STAGES 1 AND 2

Here are examples of how the child's difficulties with language and communication cause him problems in Maths.

Curriculum area: Maths	Key Stages: 1 and 2
Examples of difficulties	Suggested strategies
1. The child has difficulty understanding complex instructions.	1. Simplify your language. Give instructions one step at a time. Use objects and pictures to support the child's understanding.
2. The child is fascinated by numbers and asks the same questions over and over, interrupting the lesson.	2. Set a clear rule. Tell the child he can only ask the same thing perhaps three times. Try to set time aside for the child to be able to ask his questions.
3. The child has difficulties understanding the language of Maths. He is particularly confused when different words are used to mean the same thing (e.g. 'multiply' and 'times').	3. Use practical examples to help the words make sense. Make a collection of words that relate to each concept for the child to refer to.
4. The child isn't sure how to respond to 'why' questions.	4. Where possible, turn questions into statements with a gap for the child's answer.

SCIENCE: KEY STAGES 3 AND 4

In the final example, an older student's progress in Science is impeded by his problems with social interaction.

Curriculum area: Science	Key Stages: 3 and 4
Examples of difficulties	Suggested strategies
1. The student prefers to work alone and resists having to share a task with another student. Group activities present even more difficulties.	1. Take care in selecting partners and group members. Make the role of each partner or group member clear. Initially, the student may need to have a passive role, perhaps recording results. Gradually equip him to be able to take a more active role.
2. The student fails to show due regard for the safety of himself and others.	2. This area involves imagining the consequences of actions which students with Asperger syndrome will find difficult. It will be important to spell out in the clearest way the possible consequences of different actions. Checking procedures need to be taught and built in as routines.
3. The student is unable to ask for help in lessons.	3. First teach him to recognise that he is stuck. Specifically teach him how to ask for the help he needs. Because he cannot put himself in your shoes, he may not realise that you have the information he needs.

Examinations, tests and arrangements

Howell (2004) identifies potential difficulties for pupils on the autism spectrum in relation to tests and examinations. They can lead to particularly raised anxiety levels because:

- Exams are an unknown quantity.
- Exams mean a change in routine.
- Study leave and revision present challenges.

Additionally, the physical constraints of examinations may present problems such as large unfamiliar exam halls, the presence of large numbers of other pupils and time constraints on performance. Therefore, throughout the child's school career an evaluation should be made of the specific arrangements necessary to support the child's access and to optimise his performance.

It is particularly important that access arrangements for examinations and qualifications at Key Stage 4 are given early consideration. Application for GCSE access arrangements now have to be made online. One application can cover up to 26 months from the date of the assessment. A range of strategies may be put in place but for some of these evidence of assessments in a diagnostic report by an educational psychologist or specialist teacher must have been completed within 26 months of the final exam for which access arrangements are requested. In all cases, evidence of need from an appropriately qualified professional, together with evidence of the pupil's normal way of working and the history of need and provision must be kept on file (which may be selected for inspection).

Particular features of the Asperger syndrome learning style may indicate the need for specific access arrangements including:

- handwriting difficulties (e.g. illegibility, poor writing speed and reluctance to write);
- comprehension difficulties (e.g. literal understanding);
- attention difficulties;
- lack of awareness of time;
- social issues.

Strategies likely to be helpful for pupils with Asperger syndrome include the use of:

- reader;
- scribe;
- word processor;
- extra time (up to 25 per cent, ten per cent may be appropriate);
- oral language modifier (OLM).

These would all require a specialist diagnostic report.

Other strategies which may be helpful include:

- modified papers;
- supervised rest breaks;
- transcript;
- prompter;
- separate examination room.

READER
A reader may be provided where a standardised reading score below 85 in accuracy, speed or comprehension is evidenced. (This is not allowed in papers assessing reading, such as English Language). Or the candidate may read aloud.

SCRIBE
A scribe may be provided where there is evidence of illegibility due to poor writing, incomprehensible grammar, below average spelling, below average speed of writing.

WORD PROCESSOR
A word processor is often a preferred alternative for pupils with Asperger syndrome who have poor handwriting, below average speed and/or who may be reluctant to write but flourish when given word processor access. Again this requires evidence of normal practice.

EXTRA TIME
Extra time can be provided where a specialist assessment report indicates clear evidence of need. Usually up to 25 per cent extra time is considered, but more additional time

could be requested where there is evidence of substantially below average speed of processing.

ORAL LANGUAGE MODIFIER (OLM)

An OLM can be made available for pupils with a below average (i.e. below 85) score for reading comprehension. It may suit pupils with Asperger syndrome, although oral modification requires quite a sophisticated level of skill, and training should be undertaken by the OLM. Modified papers may, therefore, be more suitable.

MODIFIED PAPERS

Modified papers can be accessed online and can be provided for pupils with comprehension difficulties such as those experienced in Asperger syndrome. Evidence is not required.

SUPERVISED REST BREAKS

Supervised rest breaks are suitable for candidates who have concentration problems or who may experience extreme stress. They can be taken in the exam room or outside if supervised.

TRANSCRIPT

A transcript of illegible or difficult to read handwriting can be produced by a subject teacher. No specific evidence is required for this arrangement.

PROMPTER

A prompter can be helpful for pupils who have little sense of time or lose concentration easily to keep the candidate focused on the question. Prompts can be verbal (e.g. saying the candidate's name) or visual (e.g. on cards), which could be particularly helpful for pupils with Asperger syndrome. No specific evidence is required.

SEPARATE EXAMINATION ROOM

A separate examination room does not require specific evidence, but this is often very helpful for pupils with Asperger syndrome.

Towards the end of Key Stage 3, the school SENCO will need to consider the results of standardised tests, specialist support evidence, IEPs and the history of provision for the pupil with Asperger syndrome, and then to consult with subject teachers, parents and the pupil in order to inform the school's examination officer of the access arrangements which will be required. Timely further assessments can then be organised as necessary and appropriate evidence collected.

Detailed information is provided in 'Access Arrangements, Reasonable Adjustments and Special Consideration' published by the JCQ. (Advice given here relates to 08/09 publication and would need to be updated).

Non-curricular areas

For many children with Asperger syndrome, it is not the curriculum that causes them the most difficulty. Rather, it is the non-curricular areas (e.g. assembly, playtime and lunch break) which they find the most challenging and difficult to cope with. It is their behaviour at these times which may first raise their teachers' concerns.

The following are examples of these behaviours:

- Ricky, in a reception class, would scream whenever he was asked to sit amongst the other children on the carpet.
- At playtime, Bryony would continuously walk around the perimeter of the playground, following the lines of the netball court. She would have nothing to do with the other children.
- David spent all his playtime on tiptoe at the edge of the school yard, his eyes fixed on the town hall clock.
- In assembly, Simon showed no awareness of the other 200 children. He saw no reason why he couldn't talk one-to-one with the head teacher.

Teachers may feel that their chief role is to teach the curriculum, and feel less secure in their ability to develop a child's interpersonal skills – particularly to the extent required for a child with Asperger syndrome. The following information aims to give starting points for intervention by offering examples of good practice in a variety of situations.

Assembly

Assembly can be a difficult time. There is hustle and bustle on the way into the hall, and on the way back. Lots of children sit closely together. The rules seem different from those which operate in the classroom, and are difficult for a child with Asperger syndrome to understand. An adult stands at the front asking rhetorical questions and sometimes shouting.

Strategies to help the child with Asperger syndrome cope with assembly include:

- Consider whether going into assembly is a priority for the child, particularly if he is very anxious. Initially, the time may be better spent in a quiet one-to-one activity, focusing on other targets. When the child is generally more relaxed, he can gradually be brought into assembly.
- Clearly explain the rules which apply in assembly, using visual prompts to reinforce them.
- Allow the child to sit at the edge of a group, rather than in the middle. Make sure he has sufficient personal space to feel comfortable.
- Praise the child for sitting quietly.
- Encourage another child to take on a buddy role, prompting and offering guidance.
- Investigate the possible causes of difficulty. Consider a Social Story. (For example, Finley thought everyone was staring at him when actually they were just gazing around the hall.)

Playtime

For the majority of children, playtime is the best part of the school day, but children with Asperger syndrome may dread playtime. Playtime is unstructured. Children are noisy and boisterous. There are no rules.

Social pairings and groups develop. Teachers often report that the child with Asperger syndrome has no friends and is a loner in the playground. Playtime presents opportunities for developing the child's social skills, whilst accepting his need to relax in his own way.

Strategies to help the child with Asperger syndrome cope with playtime include:

- Setting a playground ethos in which collaboration is encouraged.
- Accepting that the child with Asperger syndrome may need to be on his own at playtime as respite from the social demands of the classroom.
- Organising simple, structured, social games where each individual's role is obvious. Prompt the child to join in.
- Encouraging the child to observe the activities taking place in the playground. Talk them through. Find one activity which appeals to the child and, with peer support, encourage him to join in.
- Teaching the child useful opening lines which will help him to initiate a conversation. Children with Asperger syndrome often want to be a part of things but they don't know how. (For example, James would carry a football programme in his pocket and approach other boys, asking if they wanted to look at it with him.)

Moving around school

In the primary school there is movement, and the potential for confusion, at certain key times of day. This increases enormously at secondary school when there is often wholesale movement at the end of each lesson. These times can be stressful for the child with Asperger syndrome simply because of the sheer volume of children moving through a small area. Additional anxiety is generated in the secondary school by the need to find the right room in a huge building.

Strategies to help the child with Asperger syndrome cope with moving around the school include:

- initially staggering the child's arrival/departure so that the volume of traffic is less overwhelming;
- arranging visits to the secondary school prior to transfer to give the child the opportunity to learn its layout;
- establishing a network of buddies or a Circle of Friends who will be available to act as guides;
- consider using a visual cue or signal for the child to indicate to the teacher that he needs to leave the classroom area.

In the dining room

Dining rooms can be noisy and very socially demanding. Children are expected to eat publicly alongside six or eight other children. Most school lunch times involve queueing – an activity which many children with Asperger syndrome find difficult to tolerate.

Strategies to help the child with Asperger syndrome cope with the school dining room include:

- Establishing clear rules, reinforced by visual prompts.
- Role playing lunchtime routines in a quiet, empty dining room.
- Consider allowing the child to be at the front or the end of the queue rather than in the middle of everyone. This will feel less threatening to the child.

- Alerting lunchtime supervisors to the child's difficulties and the strategies which are being used.
- Teaching simple conversation skills to help him join in with the others on his table.

Asking for help and solving problems

'Miss! How do you do this?' Most children readily ask for help when they are unsure. Children with Asperger syndrome find this particularly difficult to do for a combination of reasons:

- Children with Asperger syndrome have difficulty with problem solving, combining the elements of a task to help guide them towards a solution. Asking for someone's help is one element in the problem-solving process. They don't necessarily see the link between the problem and outside help.
- Because children with Asperger syndrome are impaired in their ability to recognise that others have different points of view, they may not realise that someone else has a solution to their problem.

Unfortunately, this behaviour can be misinterpreted as laziness or lack of motivation, thinking the child is avoiding work rather than unable to get on with it.

Strategies to help the child with Asperger syndrome ask for the help he needs include:

- Having an awareness of which tasks cause the child particular difficulty.
- Trying to work alongside the child if he is having difficulty in interpreting a task. Do the task yourself and draw his attention to what you are doing. Let him have a turn at doing part of the task. Gradually reduce your input until the child can work independently.
- Getting the child to reflect on his own learning when he has completed a task. Talk through what he did and how he did it.
- Specifically, teaching (with a visual signal) the child how to recognise when he is stuck, and how to ask for help. (For example, Damien had two flags, one which said 'I'm doing OK', the other saying, 'I'd like some help please'. He stood the appropriate flag on his desk.)

Working with others

Teachers expect children to be in close proximity to others at several times during the school day. They may be unaware of the stress this may cause the child with Asperger syndrome who has such difficulty in relating to others. The child with Asperger syndrome has little or no awareness of others' feelings or of the impact of his own behaviour on others. They may passively accept the presence of other children, but some children become tense just because someone is sitting too near them. Contact will be one-sided – from the other child to them – but rarely reciprocated. Increasingly, children in school are expected to work collaboratively with a partner or a small group. With careful planning and preparation, the child with Asperger syndrome can be included in these activities.

Strategies to help the child with Asperger syndrome to work with others include:

- Having an awareness of the level of social contact that the child can tolerate without becoming anxious.

- Initially allowing the child to sit on the edge of a group activity, perhaps with a support assistant between him and the other children.

- Considering seating arrangements. The child may feel more comfortable if the next child sits diagonally across from him rather than beside him.

- Setting up simple turn-taking tasks once the child will tolerate sitting near others. Set up turns at first just with the support assistant and later involve another child. The support assistant can finally back off, encouraging the child to work with his partner.

- Using the child's own special skills or interests, perhaps getting him to show a partner how to do something on the computer.

- Clearly defining and teaching each person's role in a group task or team activity, removing uncertainty for the child with Asperger syndrome.

School life becomes easier for children with Asperger syndrome when the adults around them recognise the extent to which social demands result in stress. Intervention and support in this area pays dividends in terms of academic attainments since stress impedes learning.

Transitions

A child or young person with Asperger syndrome goes through many transitions during their time in the education system and these transitions occur at a number of levels. Perhaps the most obvious transitions are those during which the child moves from phase to phase: from pre-school into primary school; from primary school into secondary school; and from secondary school into college. For these major transitions to happen smoothly, careful planning is needed. Key people to be involved in this planning should include staff from both settings, parents and, preferably, the child himself. Ideally, a detailed transition plan will be drawn up and agreed. This plan should outline who will take responsibility for each action.

To inform this plan, key information needs to be gathered including:

- the pupil's likes and dislikes;

- the things which motivate the pupil;

- details of how the pupil shows early signs of stress and anxiety;

- information about what works best to calm the pupil when he's upset;

- how the pupil communicates his needs;

- any particular sensitivities the pupil may have;

- how the pupil reacts to change;

- the strategies which have been tried and have worked;

- the strategies which have **not** worked and should be avoided.

Case study

John, Ollie, George and Ben all have Asperger syndrome. They attended different primary schools where each received regular input from the local authority's support service for pupils on the autism spectrum. They were all due to move into Year 7 at the same secondary school.

The advisory teacher coordinated the writing of individual plans for each boy together with parents, key staff and the boys themselves. Each boy was helped to fill in a 'Moving up' booklet which helped to highlight things to look forward to and factors which might cause stress.

A programme of induction visits for the four boys together was arranged during the summer term. The high school's inclusion staff were involved in supporting the boys during these visits and each boy was assigned a peer mentor from an older year group. Specific activities on these visits included trying the canteen and finding how to get from one teaching area to another. They were reassured to find that they needn't go out in the playground at breaks, but could go to 'lunchtime club' in the learning support area.

When they entered secondary school in the September all the boys settled well.

Other, less major, transitions should not be overlooked. Within a single school day, a child with Asperger syndrome has many transitions to cope with. During a typical day in secondary school, the pupil is likely to have to face the following:

- finding the way from home to school and perhaps dealing with a school bus or public transport;
- finding the way from school entrance to the correct classroom along a bustling corridor;
- registering;
- changing classrooms several times;
- having a number of different teachers who each have their own teaching style and expectations;
- taking breaks (what happens on wet days?);
- negotiating the canteen, its queues and its noise at lunchtime;
- having PE;
- going to assembly and dealing with the pressures of being in a large crowded room.

Even during a single lesson there are many transitions a pupil has to deal with, perhaps:

- queuing outside the classroom door;
- entering the room and deciding where to sit (some teachers have a seating plan, others don't);
- waiting for pupils to settle down and the teacher to begin the lesson;
- listening to the introduction of the lesson and trying to understand what the teacher wants the pupils to do;

- getting necessary equipment;
- beginning the task;
- perhaps listening to further explanations;
- finishing the task;
- having a plenary session;
- writing down the homework;
- listening to the end of lesson;
- packing away equipment;
- exiting the classroom.

Case study

Stefan had great difficulty organising himself and the things he needed for each lesson. He found it very stressful to make his way along the bustling corridor to each lesson. Trying to avoid other people, he would often arrive late for his next lesson. He also got worried about not being able to write down the homework assignment quickly enough.

His parents helped him by showing him how to use his school planner each evening to tell him which books and kit he would need to pack for the next day. They also bought him a bag which was divided into a number of separate sections. This helped to reduce the chance of all his belongings becoming muddled up together.

Stefan was given a digital voice recorder so that he could record the teacher explaining the homework tasks. In addition, each teacher agreed to release him from class five minutes before the others so that his passage to the next lesson would be smooth.

The stress of transition times can be minimised if anxiety-provoking situations are anticipated and strategies put in place. Pupils who feel safe and secure have more of their mental and emotional resources available for learning.

Summary

- Start from the child's level.
- Attempt to see the world from the child's point of view.
- Adapt the school environment to facilitate the child's learning.
- Consult and collaborate with parents as well as professionals.
- Consider specific interventions to develop the child's skills in social interaction, social communication, social imagination and flexible thinking.
- Become familiar with the underlying psychological explanations of the child's learning style.

Behavioural intervention

The core difficulties and implications for behaviour

The core difficulties of Asperger syndrome are exactly those which could be expected to lead to behavioural difficulties for a child.

The notion proposed by the TEACCH system – that people with autism operate from within a different 'culture' – is illuminating. In this sense, children on the autism spectrum do not 'speak our language', do not understand our ways of communicating and may need an 'interpreter'. They may be seen as having extreme difficulty at times in 'cracking the code' of our way of being.

Specific areas of difficulty which impact on behaviour are as follows:

Decoding people

Simon Baron-Cohen (1996) describes 'mind-reading' as a game of social chess, involving constantly changing strategies in the negotiation of 'social plot and counter plot'. He goes on to point out that the way we play this social chess is intuitive; it does not, typically, involve laborious logical reasoning. In contrast, for the child with Asperger syndrome, interpreting the behaviour of others is difficult, even at the simplest level. For example, when Patrick, looking at an illustration of a crying child, was asked to talk about the picture, he named the tears 'drips of water', totally missing the emotional point. So, in the classroom situation, the significance of the stern look, the raised eyebrow and other subtle, non-verbal means of classroom management are lost on the child with Asperger syndrome.

The young child with Asperger syndrome simply cannot see himself as a member of a group and may turn his back on the teacher at storytime or trample over another child to get to what he wants, but there is no intention to ignore or hurt others. The frustrated class teacher, seeking advice on such a child, will often refer to 'extreme non-compliance'.

Encoding self

Through understanding others we understand ourselves and vice versa. The child with Asperger syndrome misses out on the creation of an inner life as well as a social life. For example, a simple request to one child to 'give me a smile' was met by him putting his fingers to the corners of his mouth, lifting them up. Another child found it hard to understand what made him upset and why he cried. He used to try to push his tears back in. He felt out of control, and this only added to his distress.

Figure 6.1 Give me a smile

For Jordan and Powell (1995), the child with such extreme difficulties in understanding and interpreting emotion is unable to give meaning to his own participation in events in his life, lacking a sense of 'experiencing self'.

Social imagination

Social imagination gives us the ability to pose alternatives in the mind, including alternative images or interpretations of our own behaviour and the behaviour of others and alternative courses of action. For example, Alex was a six-year-old boy who usually ignored other children in the playground. For two consecutive days, a little girl had included him in her game – much to the delight of his support assistant. On the third day, when the same friendly girl asked him to play, he brusquely replied, 'No! Go away', neither anticipating the effect this would have on her, nor registering her response when it occurred.

Cracking the language code

Instructions given to the whole class are frequently not noticed by the child with Asperger syndrome, who doesn't recognise they apply to him too. Conversely, if the child with Asperger syndrome is sitting amongst his classmates while the teacher talks to them all, he will very often shout out responses as if the teacher was just talking to him. This behaviour is not deliberately disruptive, but it may appear to be. For example, as the children sat quietly at their tables in the nursery, waiting for the teacher to begin reading a poem, Callum called out, 'I'm not staying for lunch today, I'm having lunch with Mummy.' 'Yes, that's right', the teacher replied, and again tried to begin to read the poem. Callum interrupted again, 'I'm not staying for lunch today, I'm having lunch with Mummy.' The teacher acknowledged his comment, and again began to read. Callum's deep monotone again boomed out, 'I'm not staying . . .' 'Now, I'd like you to do your exercises', said the teacher, half way through the English lesson. Bryn got down on the floor and started to perform physical jerks. He was not trying to be funny. In another example, Peter was playing a game where the children were asked to be a particular number. He began to cry, 'I don't want to be a number, I'm not a number.'

Rigidity and rule-bound behaviour

This may arise from the inability to abstract and infer simple social rules from the problems with central coherence described earlier. It can lead to episodes of confrontation. For example, Alex did not see why he should work through endless similar Maths examples; he had done one, and he knew how to do the others. Doing more of the same seemed pointless to him.

Exclusive interests and obsessions

Certain behaviours or interests appear to take over at times at the expense of learning, social interaction or other activities. But the reason for stopping or postponing such behaviours is usually ours, not the child's. For the child, they are intrinsically rewarding, and it can be difficult to find a competing reward.

Compulsivity, perseveration and perfectionism

These features can lead to the child not being able to stop an activity or, conversely, not being able to start. This can be seen as uncooperative behaviour. For example, Imran would write a word, but become frustrated because it was not as perfect as the printed word in his book. He would rub it out and rewrite it over and over again. He was never satisfied with what he produced and never completed a page of work.

Integrated learning

Minutiae are attended to, and concrete detail required, but generalisation does not occur. Concepts are not derived from facts. The child may excel in one aspect of a subject, but be unable to tackle other aspects. For example, Clyde, aged nine, could multiply and divide four-digit numbers. He was given a Maths test in which the calculations were presented as problems to solve. He wept bitterly, unable to understand what to do, saying, 'You didn't teach me these. I can't do them.'

Sensory experience

In autism, hypersensitivity or hyposensitivity may occur visually and aurally, sometimes with the additional involvement of taste, smell and touch. This can lead to extreme reactions, modulating difficulties and overreactions to relatively subtle changes. Though perhaps less obvious in Asperger syndrome, children can be extra sensitive in this way.

Motor control

There may be poor coordination and difficulty with handwriting. This can make a child vulnerable to teasing in the playground and PE and it may lead to the avoidance of writing tasks in the classroom. For example, Russell refused to write. His support assistant arranged for him to use the computer instead and he went on to experiment with a variety of writing styles.

Approaches to managing behaviour in Asperger syndrome

Asperger syndrome: 'quintessentially a disorder of human relationships'.

(Tantam 1987)

Behaviour difficulties occur in the social arena, which is exactly the area in which people with Asperger syndrome experience most problems. The rules of social behaviour are invented, often subtle, changed by negotiation and unwritten. Although we teach the skill of reading step by step, we expect children to acquire the skills of social interaction without explicit teaching. Children with Asperger syndrome find this very difficult.

All behaviour serves a purpose: it is functional, or at least it is intended to be. In order to analyse the functions of any particular behaviour, we need to put aside moral perspective or pet beliefs and refrain from imposing intuitive or subjective interpretations on the behaviour of others.

In order to intervene in an attempt to change the behaviour of children with Asperger syndrome, it is necessary to understand the function or purpose of the behaviour from the point of view of the child. It is important to look at the behaviour and the events surrounding it as if through an Asperger 'lens'.

Simple observation, recording and behavioural intervention are not enough, since the trigger to behaviour may be almost undetectable and the function the behaviour is serving may be quite unexpected from our point of view.

For example, Ryan, aged five, suddenly began banging on the living room wall while his parents were talking to the specialist teacher. The conversation paused, Ryan's parents looked bewildered at this sudden inexplicable loud banging. The teacher noticed a faint sound of banging coming from the house next door. Alert to the frequent sensory hypersensitivity of children within the autism spectrum, she was able to tune in to the world from Ryan's point of view and to understand the trigger of his behaviour.

Before reading the behaviour of the child with Asperger syndrome, it helps to widen the field of our perception. We need to check which lens we are using and pose likely possibilities from the point of view of the Asperger lens on the world. Use of the Asperger lens in appraising behavioural difficulties occurring in children with Asperger syndrome

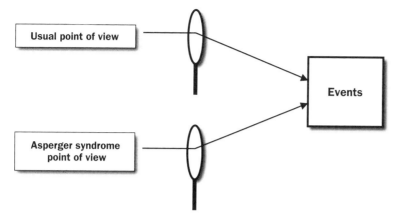

Figure 6.2 The Asperger lens of interpretation

helps to locate the source of the difficulty and to determine appropriate and, therefore, effective intervention.

The case studies which follow demonstrate how this applies.

Case studies

Case study 1

Sam:	Sam continuously rolls a pencil rapidly and noisily between his hands – distracting the other children in his primary class.
Theory:	● Use the child's obsession as a reward, rather than trying to eliminate it.
Original intervention:	● Had the aim of eliminating the pencil-rolling behaviour. ● Rewards were offered, but were ineffective.
But:	**What would the Asperger lens show us?** ● Pencil-rolling behaviour is obsessive. ● To some extent it is necessary. **New intervention** ● Use pencil-rolling behaviour as a reward. ● Sam is allowed to roll his pencil during transition times, when children are moving about and the classroom is noisier.

Case study 2

Philip: It is 9 a.m. Philip is wrapped round the gatepost at his secondary school entrance. He says he can't walk.

Theory:
- Develop alternative skills.
- Build self-esteem.
- Remove the source of difficulty.
- Reduce stress.
- Re-establish cooperation.

Original intervention:
- Fellow pupils try to pull Philip off the gatepost and drag him into school.
- Teachers quiz him about where the pain is.

But:

What would the Asperger lens show us?
- Philip experiences motor difficulties.
- He is not good at PE and the teacher is not empathic.
- Today the first lesson is PE.

New intervention
- Liaison and planning with senior staff.
- In the short term, providing an alternative to PE, while re-establishing school attendance and reducing stress.
- Giving Philip the opportunity to teach a less able pupil computer skills – raising his self-esteem and confidence.
- Offering staff (including the PE teacher) in-service training.

Case study 3

Connor: Whenever Connor sees a baby, he hits it. This causes particular problems at the end of the school day, when many of the mums are waiting with babies in pushchairs.

Theory:
- Use of rules and structured environment.
- Direct teaching of empathy.

Original intervention:
- A behaviour support teacher attempts to counsel Connor.
- They make a scrapbook about babies and the teacher explains how vulnerable they are.
- He tries to get Connor to reflect on what he was like as a baby.
- He becomes *more* obsessed with hitting babies.

But: **What would the Asperger lens show us?**

- Connor lacks the empathy and imagination to understand how a baby feels, and how limited its communication is.
- He is angered by babies' crying, and is possibly hypersensitive to loud, unexpected sound.

New intervention

- Connor is given the rule: No hitting babies.
- He leaves school by a different door, no longer confronted by a row of prams.
- Work on developing empathy is carried out:

 (a) in school, by his support assistant (e.g. he is taught not to laugh if someone falls over in the playground, but to ask if they are alright);
 (b) at home – he is rewarded for not shouting if his grandma coughs, having been given a clear rule.

Case study 4

Oliver: Prompted by fellow pupils, and to their great amusement, 13-year-old Oliver was producing smutty notes on a school computer, and handing round copies. He quoted some of the overtly sexual statements to female members of staff.

Theory:
- Identify gaps in knowledge and skills and structure the environment.

Original intervention:
- Staff express shock and consternation.
- Warning of exclusion if behaviour continues.
- A set of behavioural targets and a recording system are introduced.

But: **What would the Asperger lens show us?**

- Oliver is naive about sexual matters.
- He is anxious to have friends and is pleased that the other boys are laughing.
- He doesn't realise that the boys are laughing at him; he thinks they are now his friends.

New intervention

- The material is taken off the word processor.

- Explanations are given about acceptable language and behaviour in sexual matters.
- Oliver's social unease is recognised.
- His wish to have friends is addressed.
- Oliver's mum is involved in discussions about the need to talk to him about the nature and implications of Asperger syndrome.
- A modified behavioural plan is introduced, focusing on just two achievable targets:

    (a) completing classwork to the teacher's satisfaction;
    (b) bringing the correct equipment to the lesson.

Case study 5

Adam: Aged six years, Adam is noisy and uncooperative. He has 'deliberately' broken the computer.

Theory:
- Stress reduction.
- Structured environment.

Original intervention:
- Teacher rebukes Adam, frequently raising her voice to him in the classroom.

But: **What would the Asperger lens show us?**
- Adam is in a very cramped and crowded classroom, with a desk next to the musical instrument shelf – he turns round and uses them to make a noise.
- Adam has a loud, monotone voice with which he calls out in class. He is unaware of the disruptive effect this has on others.
- He is unnerved by his teacher's frequently raised voice.
- As his stress level rises, he becomes more noisy, less cooperative and less controlled in his behaviour.

New intervention
- The TEACCH principles for organising the classroom environment are explained to his teacher.
- The musical instruments are placed elsewhere.
- Instead of shouting at Adam across the classroom, his teacher is encouraged to give him instructions and information via the support assistant – his interpreter.
- The teacher is offered in-service training, and given an information pack on Asperger syndrome.

Case study 6

Jeff: This secondary school boy is described as 'dangerous'. He's brought a screwdriver into school and intends to use it against boys who, he believes, are teasing and bullying him.

Theory:
- Recognise the lack of subtlety in his social interaction.
- Understand his vulnerability to teasing and bullying, and intervene to prevent it.

Original intervention:
- Staff threaten exclusion and, after investigation, find no evidence of bullying.

But:

What would the Asperger lens show us?
- A specialist teacher observes so-called 'low-level' teasing and bullying in corridors and yard, not apparent to school staff.
- Jeff has no strategies for shrugging this off or dealing with it with humour.
- He becomes angry, anxious and isolated.

New intervention
- A welfare assistant, who has been given specialist training, is provided for Jeff at break and lunchtimes. He sees her as an ally.
- He is taught specific strategies for dealing with unwanted comments and approaches.

Case study 7

Rebecca: This young girl makes inappropriate remarks to family visitors (e.g. saying, 'When are you going?' just as people arrive).

Theory:
- Provide alternative responses.

Original intervention:
- Parents are angry.
- They rebuke and criticise her.

But:

What would the Asperger lens show us?
- Rebecca has an obsession with time.
- She is unaware that her comments seem impolite.

New intervention
- Parents learn to remain calm.
- They teach her more appropriate and acceptable things to do and say (e.g. 'How long can you stay?').

The main points of the behavioural interventions include:

- To identify behaviour is not to specify need.
- All behaviours reflect interactions between events on the outside, and the world within the person, as much for the 'observer' as for the 'observed'.
- Personal interpretations of events are central to feelings experienced and motivations to behave.
- There is a requirement for observation, an open mind and empathy, along with the ability to understand and read behaviour.
- An understanding of the Asperger view of the world is essential.

Preventing behavioural difficulty

[In Asperger syndrome] most of the stress comes from living in a society where everyone is expected to conform to a set pattern.

Lynda Bannister (Mother of John)

Given the nature of their social difficulties, everyday life must be a source of great difficulty, anger and incomprehension for children with autism spectrum disorders. They are particularly prone to stress.

Donna Williams (1996), a person with Asperger syndrome, writes, 'People who are in a constant state of stress and discomfort also develop strategies to help calm themselves. For some people, this might be rocking or humming or tapping themselves. For others, this might be carrying something around with them.' She links this constant stress to sensory hypersensitivity and the effects of environmental overload in her own case.

Levels of stress

Writing about her then ten-year-old son with Asperger syndrome, Lynda Bannister describes three levels of stress, as below.

At level 1, he is relatively calm and happy, eating and sleeping well, able to cope with minor irritations, reasonably sociable and giving good eye contact. In fact, a visitor to the home would be hard-pressed to tell which of the children had autism.

At level 2 though, he is 'edgy, fidgety, irritable, displaying mild symptoms of autism'. He does not sleep well, does not sit to eat a full meal, talks to himself and does detailed drawings involving maps, games, boxes and numbers. A small annoyance may produce a tantrum. Eye contact is fleeting. Whereas at level 1, John hates swearing and tells other children off if they swear, at level 2 he swears himself and giggles about it.

At level 3, Mrs Bannister describes her son as 'full blown autistic'. Violent and aggressive, he shouts and swears badly, is hyperactive and can't sleep. He won't eat, wets his bed and develops phobias. Shrugging off company of any sort, he giggles hysterically then cries bitterly. 'He draws, draws, draws, pages and pages of very detailed pictures, the higher his stress level, the more intricate the picture and the harder the picture is to understand. It is like a computer that has gone into overdrive, spilling out pages and pages of garble – "does not compute, does not compute".'

Mrs Bannister attributed this stress to her son being forced to do something which makes no sense to him – a situation in which children with Asperger syndrome often find themselves. At home the family adapts to John as an individual, not expecting him to do things he cannot do – regardless of what might be appropriate at his age. Anticipation of a difficult situation will also cause stress, as will tiredness and lack of exercise. Finally, when he is under stress, John is unable to learn socially at the same time as academically. Gaps in learning themselves cause further difficulties and lead to further stress.

Mrs Bannister's advice to her son's teacher was, 'Take the pressure out of the situation and let him be himself, all muddled up . . . Forget trying to teach him anything until he is calm enough to receive it – or you are wasting your time . . . Let him show you how and where he really is. Listen to him, let *him* lead the way, remove any pressure . . . to prevent him creating havoc for himself and others.'

Stress reduction

Specialist schools for children on the autism spectrum recognise the need to identify stress and take steps to avoid or reduce it. One school, for example, recognises the need to capitalise on the times of day when the children were likely to be both calm and alert. At these times, challenging learning activities are offered. Conversely, when the children are at their most anxious, stress-reducing activities are offered. Interestingly, the staff discovered that the children were more likely to be stressed in the earlier part of the day, and therefore start the day with the least-demanding activities. Gradually, as the day progresses, the level of challenge is increased, with stress-reducing approaches introduced again as the day draws to a close. This is in direct contrast to the approach often taken in primary schools and in schools and centres for children with behavioural difficulties where the morning is often extended to give early application to study, and more relaxed and rewarding activities begin after lunch.

Lynda Bannister refers to her son's need, at times, to get outside and run around. Again, in some specialist schools for children on the autism spectrum, emphasis is often placed on the use of vigorous physical activity.

In her autobiography, Temple Grandin (Grandin and Scariano 1986) writes, 'Doing physical labour eased my nerve attacks.'

Storm House School, run by the National Autistic Society, has developed an extensive programme of outdoor pursuits with their students (Evans 1997).

Donna Williams (1996) points to the influence of fatigue on stress, noting that, '*REAL* breaks of between five minutes to an hour in between participation can help people to sustain personal stress or information overload caused by participation. Breaks should be a peaceful and relaxing time with no non-calming and non-welcomed stimulation.' Other approaches she recommends include a lessening or absence of unnecessary stimulation, no unnecessary touching and the provision of gentle, quiet, steady and calming sounds.

The judicious use of stress-releasing activities within the mainstream setting can help prevent behavioural disturbance. For example, Ashley's teachers were worried at how he would cope with the school building extension since he is easily distracted and unnerved by noise. The support teacher suggested that for part of the school day during this period of disruption, Ashley should be taken out of school by his special support assistant. She was to work on a programme of independence skills, social interaction and practical Maths through trips to local shops. This served to reduce Ashley's stress, while providing useful learning experiences. The building period passed without incident.

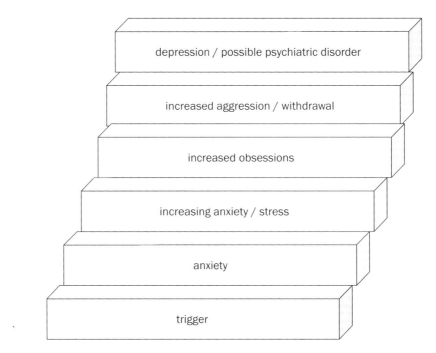

Figure 6.3 Steps in the escalation of stress

Stress, if left unrecognised, can lead to escalation in anxiety and obsessions, leading to an increase in aggressive or withdrawn behaviour with a possible onset of depression or psychiatric disorder.

A general review of the stress level of the child with Asperger syndrome is always useful if behavioural difficulties are being experienced. Steps may then be taken to improve the underlying conditions which may be causing stress and also to offer opportunities for de-stressing through relaxation or physical exercise within the context of the mainstream environment.

Vulnerability in Asperger syndrome

Mental health issues

The vulnerability of individuals with Asperger syndrome to raised levels of stress, anxiety and depression has been established in studies of children and adolescents (Kim *et al.* 2000; Bellini 2004; Wolff 1995) and adults (Tantam 1988). Ghaziuddin (2005) has provided a welcome source of information and advice in this area in his book *Mental Health Aspects of Autism and Asperger's Syndrome*. He identifies the most common types of anxiety disorder as:

- Obsessive Compulsive Disorder (OCD);
- Post Traumatic Stress Disorder (PTSD);
- School Refusal;
- Selective Mutism;
- Social Anxiety Disorder.

The prevalence of OCD in those on the autism spectrum is not known. However, there is evidence that OCD is more frequent in first-degree relatives of individuals on the autism spectrum. The presenting picture may seem confusing as compulsive rituals and/ or preoccupation with obsessive interests are integral to the autism spectrum. However, it is when these symptoms are exacerbated to a degree which causes serious concern that an additional diagnosis of OCD may need to be considered.

Case study

Cara, an eight-year-old girl with Asperger syndrome, had apparently coped with mainstream inclusion in the local primary school. When her behaviour became increasingly oppositional, the school became concerned. As she crossed the playground with her father she stopped and insisted he retrace his steps several times as she became increasingly angry and upset.

CAMHS [The Child and Adolescent Mental Health Services] staff were involved and a placement arranged at a local specialist school. Cara's rigid, controlling behaviour continued to be extreme and began to evidence compulsive elements; Cara needing to complete many rituals. She refused to dress at all and would become wildly distressed and enraged. Multi-agency collaboration resulted in the CAMHS psychiatrist diagnosing OCD in addition to AS. Prescribed medication, additional staffing support from the local authority and a residential place together with excellent input at the school and home liaison produced radical progress. Cara is now an able, communicative teenager considering reducing medication and a university career though, in the face of much social awareness training, has boldly announced, 'I don't just want to be a well-groomed autistic person, you know'.

Crucially, with regard to the possibility of mental health difficulties occurring, Ghaziuddin advises that it is important 'to maintain a high index of suspicion, especially when there is a history of a recent change in the level of functioning, often during adolescence'.

Behavioural symptoms including mood swings, hyperactivity, aggressive behaviour should not be ignored as incidental aspects of the overall syndrome.

Depression can easily be missed and includes indicative features such as crying spells, disturbed sleep and appetite and increased social withdrawal as in the general population. Features noted by Ghaziuddin as specific to the autism spectrum include:

- increase in level of isolation and withdrawal;
- increase in ritualistic behaviours;
- change in quality of fixations and obsessions;
- increased irritability, loss of temper and possibly physical aggression;
- regression of skills;
- increased suspicion of others.

Anti-depressant medication may be prescribed and psychological intervention including Cognitive Behaviour Therapy (CBT) can be helpful.

It is important for school staff to be aware of these potentially increased levels of vulnerability in their pupils with Asperger syndrome where unusual levels of stressed, anxious, depressed, angry or aggressive behaviour are of concern to school staff. Family consultation should be sought with the involvement of the specialist support teacher, educational psychologist, school nurse and members of the local CAMHS team. Parents can themselves seek referral to the CAMHS team via their GP.

Good Practice Guidance (2002 DfES, DoH) advises that the autism spectrum-friendly school should develop communication networks between the LEA and Health and Social Services departments so that there is a three-way flow of information regarding individual children on the autism spectrum and a three-way flow of up-to-date information regarding autism spectrum policy and practice.

Bullying

Bullying can have a destructive and harmful impact on the lives of children and young people. It not only affects those being bullied, but also those who bully. The definition of bullying used by the Department for Children, Schools and Families in *Safe to Learn* (2007) is: 'Behaviour by an individual or group, usually repeated over time, that intentionally hurts another individual or group either physically or emotionally.' Bullying can lead to feelings of self-doubt, lack of confidence, low self-esteem, anxiety, depression and sometimes even suicide. Ofsted's TellUs2 survey of Years 6, 8 and 10 puts the level of bullying at 29 per cent.

Bullying and Asperger syndrome

Often children and young people on the autism spectrum will be bullied and may be perceived as bullies. Their literal understanding of language, difficulties in understanding other people (TOM), formal use of language, rigidity of thought leading to certain behaviour patterns and difficulties in forming social relationships make these children and young people susceptible to being bullied.

The total compliance to school rules, pedantic use of language and personal comments on aspects of appearance can lead to the child/young person being at risk of being bullied. For example, Lee was in his first weeks at secondary school when he spotted a group of Year 11 boys who did not have their ties tied correctly walking towards him on the corridor. He stopped them and told them the school rules regarding how ties should be worn.

The lack of empathy, lack of awareness of personal space, lack of awareness of non-verbal signals and curiosity about events (the little professor part of the condition), can lead to people perceiving the child/young person on the autism spectrum as a bully.

There are occasions when ordinary peer interaction is mistakenly interpreted by the child/young person on the autism spectrum as bullying. For example, Liam told his support assistant that he was being bullied between lessons. He was being jostled as he walked along the school corridor in between lessons. The corridor was narrow and the young people carried rucksacks with their books in from lesson to lesson. He could not see that everyone was jostled he could only see it was happening to him.

Reducing incidents of bullying

Bullying takes place in every school. Schools which have a supportive culture, where there is an emphasis on sharing responsibility and the importance of respecting the rights of everyone in the community, are the most successful in reducing bullying.

When working with a child with Asperger syndrome there are a number of actions that will help reduce incidents:

- awareness from all staff of the child/young person's individual needs;
- a risk assessment of the child/young person's interaction levels and a plan to increase skill levels and help reduce the risks;
- an environmental audit to identify places where bullying can take place away from adult oversight;
- children/young people should be involved in reducing bullying;
- peer support;
- a named person who will listen.

Strategies that can help are:

- circle time;
- Social Stories;
- Circle of Friends;
- Social and Emotional Aspects of Learning (SEAL) materials and activities;
- a 'friends' bench in the playground;
- alternative activities for lunchtime and playtime;
- social communication groups, which cover aspects of friendship.

Youth justice issues

There are a number of young people on the autism spectrum who come into contact with the youth justice system, either as a victim or a perpetrator. The system must be sensitive to the needs of the young people in order to ensure that justice is done.

There are children and young people who are victims of sexual exploitation and in some cases abuse. For example, Steven, a young boy with Asperger syndrome, was encouraged by a neighbour to come and play at his house. Whilst there, a sexual act took place. Some days later Steven disclosed this information in school and the police were informed. Steven was questioned by the officers from the Family Support Unit who dismissed his story as he did not show the expected emotions when re-telling his story.

This episode shows that children and young people with Asperger syndrome are vulnerable in a number of ways:

- lack of understanding of danger;
- lack of understanding of the implications of their actions;
- lack of understanding of how other people may interpret their behaviour;
- past experience is not generalised;
- difficulty expressing feelings;
- difficulty in understanding emotions (their own and those of others);
- difficulty with verbal and non-verbal communication;
- social naivete;
- high levels of anxiety if they do not understand what is going on around them.

Some of the obsessive behaviours that fascinate children and young people with Asperger syndrome can lead them into trouble. For example, James liked to stroke people, particularly females, across the chest. In school he had been taught to ask, 'Please can I stroke you?' in order to limit this behaviour. However, one sunny afternoon in the local park James was arrested for approaching women and asking if he could stroke them.

There are times when the desire for friends leads young people with Asperger syndrome to be the fall guy for their 'friends' misdemeanours. For example, Andrew hung out with a group of boys on his estate who were known for committing acts of anti-social behaviour. He was the one who was blamed for smashing wing mirrors on a row of cars as when asked by the police had he been involved he said, 'yes' while the others said, 'no'.

The high levels of anxiety due to a lack of understanding can be expressed in behaviours that can cause challenges. For example, Carl and his mum had a very difficult relationship. Carl did not understand Mum's need to have a break from caring for him. When being cared for outside the family home Carl would, whenever possible, run back home. His mum would become angry and not allow him in; there were times when this anger became violent and the police were called. Mum would ask the police to press charges. However, when his mum tried to drive into Carl in front of care workers and the police were called, Carl refused to press charges because, 'You don't do that to family – do you?'.

It should be recognised by those working in the criminal justice system, including police officers, that young people with Asperger syndrome are vulnerable and should be treated as such. Even though they may be very articulate, the ways in which they perceive the world are different. Consequently, they cannot follow the expected patterns of behaviour, but this does not mean they are guilty.

The aim of staff should be to:

- keep the situation calm;
- communicate in a clear, concise and simple manner that does not use technical language or sarcasm;
- use graphics or pictures to aid communication;
- prepare the person for what will happen to them (e.g. in an interview or court appearance);
- allow extra response time;
- check that lights and noises are not causing sensory overload;
- if needed, identify an advocate with an understanding of Asperger syndrome.

Structuring the school environment for prevention

A key feature of the success of the TEACCH approach to the education of children with autism is the recognition of the core difficulty of rigidity in autism. That is, that children with autism need to control their environment and adhere to rules and routines. For the children themselves, the experience may be one of being controlled, as a young university student with Asperger syndrome (Peers 1997) eloquently describes it, 'Build obsessions into goals, use obsessions in a positive way without letting them rule your life. BE IN CONTROL!!!!'

The need to control can, however, lead to a battle of wills: the teacher's need to direct versus the child's need to control.

The TEACCH system offers a way of sharing control so that issues are externalised. Here is an explicit visual and physical structure which can be read by the child so that daily life in school becomes predictable. The importance of organising the environment to compensate for the child's difficulties is outlined in Chapter 5, together with ways of adapting the environment at several levels. These methods should lead to a reduction in conflict situations and serve to reduce stress in the pupil with Asperger syndrome.

Use of rules

Because children with Asperger syndrome are often rule-bound and driven by routine, rules can be used positively to prevent behavioural difficulties.

A class teacher using the 'Rules, Praise and Ignore' approach (Madsen *et al.* 1968) will make life easier for the child with Asperger syndrome. However, the principle of explaining the rules of the situation can be extended. Activities where a teacher would assume the rules were known (e.g. the rules for 'lining up' or for 'going out to play') may need to be unpacked. Some of these are addressed in the non-curricular section of Chapter 5.

At a more subtle level, the child may need to be involved in discussion of the rules for 'getting someone's attention' or 'how the teacher gets the children's attention'. Sometimes the child with Asperger syndrome will apply the rules universally himself, telling the teacher when a child is breaking a rule or, inappropriately, telling a burly smoker on a bus that smoking is not allowed. The usefulness of rules in preventing behaviour problems is that they are neutral, allowing for an appeal to an objective standard and reducing the need for confrontation.

A non-confrontational, objective and emotionally detached approach

A battle of wills with a child with Asperger syndrome is always to be avoided since it cannot be won. The lack of negotiating skills, imagination and empathy in the child with Asperger syndrome can be evidenced as an apparent extreme stubbornness. Cajoling, threatening and showing emotion may lead to an increase in stress in the child, but not to cooperation. Calm, orderly and emotionally neutral approaches to negotiating with the child have the best chance of working.

Preparation and rehearsal

An advantage of the TEACCH approach is the degree of predictability it gives to the child's day with its use of sequenced, pictorial, diagrammatic or even written timetables. The system also allows for visible alteration of a sequence of events so that the child is not suddenly exposed to unexpected change. Sudden change produces anxiety and stress and can trigger behavioural difficulties. Wherever a change which is likely to cause any degree of anxiety can be anticipated, it is advisable to prepare the child beforehand. Role-play, cartoon conversation strips or prompt cards can be useful aids in this process.

Allowing for interests and obsessions

Very often, the obsessions or circumscribed interests which are found in children with Asperger syndrome serve as hobbies, giving positive pleasure to the child. Rather than attempting to remove these completely, it is helpful to allow the child his hobby under clearly recognised conditions. For example:

- Identified time: at breaks/lunchtime, during transitions or when given a bus ticket or coloured band.

- Identified place: on the carpet, in the story corner or when in the playground.

- Identified number: same question no more than three times or the special subject for five minutes then change topic.

Some obsessions may need to be eliminated, others not.

On arriving home from school, Matthew liked (needed?) to get a clean sheet of paper and begin to write a sequence of numbers: 1, 2, 3, 4, 5, 6 . . . and so on. He would continue well into the thousands, once reaching 42,000! A concerned teacher tried to eliminate this behaviour – a course of action which caused Matthew to become increasingly distressed, both at home and at school. His number writing had actually been serving to release tension at the end of the school day and it did no one any harm. He was subsequently allowed to continue writing numbers, and his stress reduced again.

Contrastingly, Steven liked to take hold of and bury his face in the long hair of some of the little girls in his class – a clearly unacceptable behaviour. The girls themselves carried out the programme which extinguished the behaviour by saying firmly, 'I don't like that' as they took his hands and removed them from their hair.

As Howlin and Rutter (1987) noted, obsessional activities can also be very useful in the below ways.

As reinforcers or rewards

Joshua, in the nursery, was provided with an 'object schedule'; each item was pinned in sequence to the back of a cupboard to illustrate the order of his morning. Thomas the Tank Engine was last in the sequence. If Thomas and the railway track had been brought out earlier, no other activities would have been possible.

As an inroad to more acceptable behaviours

Malcolm spent hours drawing diagrams of routes, roads and motorways. His mother started to encourage him to fill in other details, developing maps with him. This is now being used as a possible entry into fiction, with Tolkien's stories and the Narnia stories.

To facilitate social interaction

Max has been very solitary in his mainstream nursery and early years classes. Now he has more spoken language and can take turns. When he plays with the train set on the classroom playmat, other children are accepted. He has recently been involved in some joint play with the other boys, sharing the trains.

Summary

'Prevention is better than cure' – an old adage applicable in the context of Asperger syndrome.

- Structure the environment for prevention.
- Prepare for change, and use rehearsal before the real event where possible.
- Use rules positively.
- Adopt calm, objective, emotionally neutral approaches to negotiation.
- Allow for interests and obsessions, and incorporate these into plans and programmes.
- Be alert to the possibility of stress, and take steps to reduce it by removing potential stress triggers.

Specific intervention in behavioural difficulties

One of the major obstacles to solving behaviour problems can be impulsive responding on the part of the adult. A difficult situation can be made more problematic by inadvertent reinforcement of the problem behaviour. For example, four-year-old Joshua refused to come to the table to draw. The nursery nurse insisted. He ran away screaming. Allowed to take his time, and encouraged to come by another child, he eventually came to the table, but refused to pick up a pencil. The nursery nurse insisted. A screaming tantrum ensued. A pattern of behaviour was set up. Soon, pencil and paper, writing or drawing tasks acted as a cue for Joshua to start screaming.

Make a plan

In order to avoid setting up a worse secondary behaviour problem through inappropriate responses to the initial difficulty, it helps to step back and make a plan.

Step 1: Enlist support
Two heads are often better than one, and airing the problem with someone (e.g. the SENCO, a visiting support teacher, the educational psychologist or a parent) will often bring to light new aspects of the situation and a better plan may emerge.

Step 2: Look for the positives
Very often, when a child is presenting difficult behaviour, it begins to dominate our thinking and we can lose sight of his strengths, abilities and progress in other areas. A spiral of anxiety, anger and concern may develop and lead to a distorted perception of the problem. This will only make intervention more difficult. As soon as a problem behaviour begins to preoccupy the teaching focus, it is important to counteract negativity and identify possible reinforcers by building a profile of the child's strengths, interests, skills and preferred activities.

Step 3: Identify the purpose or function of the behaviour of the child
All behaviour is functional. Its purpose is to produce a result: 'My fixations reduced arousal and calmed me' (Grandin and Scariano 1986). It is not always possible to identify the function of behaviour for the person with Asperger syndrome. Careful detective work by the teacher using the Asperger lens can bring forward some useful hypotheses.

Step 4: Define the exact nature of the problem

It is useful to define the problem clearly in behavioural terms. The terms 'aggression' or 'tantrum' do not make it clear what the child actually does. Specify the actual behaviours.

Step 5: Observe and record

A useful observation tool is the STAR chart (Zarkowska and Clements 1988). This observation approach focuses attention not just on the child's behaviour but on all the surrounding events and actions. In this way, the setting conditions are outlined, triggers for the behaviours are noted, the child's actions and those of others are detailed and the results are reported.

Careful analysis of the resulting data will then often indicate a pattern of events and highlight useful starting points for intervention at the following levels:

SETTING CONDITIONS

For Philip, wrapped round the school gatepost, the anticipation of having PE first lesson provided the setting which had triggered the behaviour. It also suggested the intervention approach.

TRIGGERS

Jeff's anger was triggered by teasing, cruel remarks and gestures which were imperceptible to his subject teachers.

ACTIONS

Sam's pencil-rolling served to reduce stress and was part of his obsessive activity.

RESULTS

Oliver was given 'friendly' attention by the boys in his group when he printed sexually explicit material on the computer.

Design the programme

Careful observation against a background of understanding Asperger syndrome is the key to effective intervention in behavioural problems.

Facilitating alternative behaviour

As with any behavioural intervention programme, a positive approach is more effective in producing longer-term change than attempts to eliminate or extinguish behaviours. This is where the list of the child's strengths, interests, skills and preferred activities comes into play. Very often, obsessive interests may be used as reinforcers (as with Joshua in the nursery in the example given above).

Relating the rewards to the child

Again, the notes outlining the child's positive attributes will help in the selection of the most powerful rewards to be incorporated in the behaviour programme. For example, Max was given a coloured counter for cooperating on tasks; he could then exchange these in his TEACCH corner for sweets. Back-up rewards from home can be very powerful. For example, as a reward, Malcolm is taken out to explore new routes. However, positive intervention should *remain* positive! For example, Sebastian was given a home–school diary in which both ticks and crosses were recorded – achievements and misdemeanours. Sensitive to imperfection and failure, Sebastian would say to his support assistant, 'This is awful. I suppose you will be writing it down in the book, will you?' After a particularly difficult day, his mother burst into tears at the sight of all the crosses on the page. Exit Sebastian with the diary – which was never seen again! Rewards must be powerful, meaningful, consistent and predictable at the outset of any behavioural programmes in order to be effective. Visual representation of progress and rewards can help the child to focus (e.g. coloured tokens velcroed on a card).

Using graded change techniques

Change is difficult to cope with, particularly for children with Asperger syndrome because of the core rigidity. Change is best introduced very gradually indeed. For example, Simon screamed when taken into assembly. The support assistant initially sat with him as he played with his favourite cars outside and some distance from the hall. Over a period of time she gradually reduced the distance, moving nearer and nearer to the hall doors. Eventually Simon felt comfortable going just inside the hall. Finally, the support assistant substituted books for the cars. A social story can also be useful here. For example, Peter hated assemblies and cried and protested. Careful detective work by his support teacher identified the problem as Peter's misunderstanding of other children's behaviour; as they looked around the hall he thought they were all staring at him. A Social Story explaining the situation helped him to remain calm.

Implement, monitor and evaluate

Having designed a programme of intervention with appropriate rewards, it is important to record and monitor outcomes. Change may be gradual or immediate, and unexpected effects may occur. It is important to be able to track why and how success occurs as well as to identify possible sources of difficulty so that accurate, targeted alterations may be made to the programme. It is equally important to change only one element of a programme at a time. For example, Jon had been 'uncontrollable' in the teaching and therapy sessions at the Child Development Centre. The TEACCH approach was introduced,

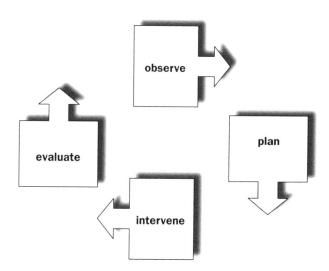

Figure 6.4 Planning cycle

and Jon learned to recognise which activity came next by looking at the sequence of pictures on his board, taking each picture away when he had completed that item. Calm prevailed. After several weeks, however, the system broke down as Jon insisted on taking the pictures from the board before even starting an activity. His teacher wondered if the activities were now too easy for him, and she considered changing some of them. She tested this hypothesis by changing just one activity, substituting a more complex toy for a simple marble game. During this activity, Jon left the picture on the board and became absorbed in the new task. This convinced his teacher that she had pinpointed the source of the difficulty. She went on to gradually introduce a range of more complex tasks.

Supertactic: Cognitive Behavioural Approaches using Visual Support

In recent years Cognitive Behaviour Therapy (CBT) has begun to be used as supportive behavioural intervention for youngsters with Asperger syndrome and autism (Lord 1995, Hare 1997, Hare and Paine 1997, Reaven and Hepburn 2003, Fitzpatrick 2004, Hare 2004, Greig and McKay 2005).

The central principle of CBT is that altering thoughts and beliefs results in changes in behaviour with an emphasis on the here and now. Specific problems are identified together with the underpinning beliefs held. Changing those beliefs by proposing alternative explanations can lead to changes in behaviour. Rather than directly challenging the person's beliefs the evidence for that belief is challenged and together alternative interpretations and beliefs are constructed. This has the advantage for people on the autism spectrum of avoiding direct confrontation and treating problems in a relatively detached and formalised way.

The kinds of strategies involved include self-monitoring, debriefing sessions and social problem solving.

Psychologists using CBT with individuals with Asperger syndrome have attended to the effectiveness of visual information in developing the approach.

Greig and McKay (2005) developed a highly engaging programme based around a comic strip character with the 'homunculus', or little man cartoons representing mental states. Moran (2005) devised a technique based on personal construct psychology called 'Drawing the Ideal Self' to draw out the child's perspective on events and possible solutions. This basically involves child and therapist in drawing the kind of person the child would not like to be and exploring the contrast with the kind of person the child would like to be, finally linking the two sets of drawings with a rating scale enabling the child to plot progress and goals.

Teachers supporting children in a range of educational settings have similarly been highly innovative in using visual techniques to support problem solving.

Self-monitoring of emotions and behaviours is the focus of 'The Incredible 5-Point Scale' (Buron and Curtis 2003). This approach involves the use of colours and numbers 'to break down a variety of behaviours into concrete points to help your student or child better understand what it is you are asking of him'. A scale can be constructed with the student to help monitor anxiety, anger, stress or behaviours such as shouting, touching and greeting. The technique capitalises on the use of visual information which is so supportive for youngsters on the autism spectrum. It is also used alongside Social Stories (Gray 2002) and also known as Social Autopsy.

Debriefing sessions may be carried out verbally but usually benefit from the support of visual information either in written form or using 'Comic Strip Conversations'. A lovely example of this approach occurred in a hearing-impaired unit visited by one of the authors where the young man in question, diagnosed with Asperger syndrome as well as a severe hearing impairment, would arrive back at base enraged at some incident on the playground or corridor or in another lesson. He would be speechless with anger. Even when calm he found it difficult to sequentially explain events and emotions. The teacher in charge of the unit, knowing he liked to draw, kept a stock of paper with lined boxes on it ready so that he could draw the sequence of events using thought bubbles. The approach proved to be calming, informative and a starting point for looking at what might have been a more useful response.

Julie Prentice, an Outreach Support Teacher in the North East, also recommends the computer version, 'Bubble Dialogue'. It is a programme which can be used to set up a scenario for a young person to practise their communication for a social situation. As with Comic Strip Conversations, a picture of the situation with speech and thought bubbles is used to depict the situation. Situations which have gone wrong can be reassessed using this visual computer-based strategy.

Michelle Garcia Winner, a Californian Speech and Language Pathologist, in her book *Thinking About You, Thinking About Me* (2002) develops Social Mapping as a way of schematically exploring what is already happening in a situation and what could happen instead. Tables are drawn up for 'expected behaviours' and 'unexpected behaviours'.

Case studies: integrating strategies to promote behavioural change

Case study 1: Luke

Burons' 5-point scale for self-monitoring anger offers a colourful, visual chart to support the youngster with Asperger syndrome in recognising mounting levels of anger and then taking pre-planned action. Harries (2008) introduced it to a 12-year-old in his class who persistently hit out at other pupils, often in the playground when other staff were supervising. It was agreed that when Luke's anger reached level 3, he would approach a member of staff for support in tackling the problem thus returning to the calm of level 1. Staff in school were all made aware of the procedure; charts were completed in both Welsh and English as Welsh is Luke's first language. Within days, Luke was hauled before the headmaster, having thumped another pupil. When reminded that he should have sought staff support to get back to level 1 before hitting out, Luke replied that he hadn't needed to: when he thumped the other pupil he felt a lot less angry and that got him back to level 1!

A combination of strategies was needed. Luke would need a powerful motivator to hold back from hitting out when his anger reached level 3 – a reward for not doing so. Discussions about angry feelings and what could be done to manage them were held with the class group. Luke identified his strategy as writing his feelings down at the computer, a preferred activity. Together with Luke, Deiniol, his teacher, gained his agreement that next time his anger hit level 3 he would leave the situation and go to the computer, where he would be allowed to spend ten minutes writing down how he felt. This combination of strategies produced a marked improvement. Luke was subsequently able to access more rewarding feedback from staff and peers, with the threat of violence removed Harries (2008).

Case study 2: David

David, a six-year-old described as 'difficult, cocky and unwilling to learn', was being assessed for a possible diagnosis on the autism spectrum. His shouting out and general noise levels made classroom life difficult. When the support service teacher looked at data from ABC observations she had elicited from staff, non-compliance was clearly an issue and staff had interpreted this as naughtiness!

Direct discussion with David produced some interesting responses. When Helen, the support service teacher, asked him his class teacher's name, he gave the name of the previous year's teacher, 'No, that was your other teacher in Class 1. That lady there [pointing to the current teacher] is now your teacher', said Helen. 'Really, well I had no idea!' was the reply. The visual strategy employed consisted of a chart with support staff and teachers' photos on it displayed in a hierarchical order so that David had a visual prompt for who was in charge. Additionally, staff were advised to always say his name when addressing the class. They were advised to use closed questions and avoid asking whether he wanted to do something, but to give clear instructions. The effect on David's behaviour was dramatic and instant.

Again, enquiries produced interesting information relating to David's noise levels. When class noise levels rose David, unaware of the teacher's gestures to stop, explained that he was increasing his noise level to help – maintaining the level of noise in the classroom!

A combination of a 'Noise Scale' and Social Stories was then used to help him monitor his own behaviour and to explain that the other children's behaviour was not his concern. The whole class was included in the approach. A Noise Scale was constructed with a row of numbers 0 to 10, with a quiet face at one end and a shouting face at the other, together with an arrow and a chart. The teacher played a game of noise levels with the children. They gauged the score for each noise level and decided what would be acceptable for each session of the day. A 'noise monitor' was then appointed to tell the teacher if the noise became too loud in a session –volunteers for the post were numerous! David himself had a personalised daily timetable with a place for the agreed level of noise for each activity. It also included breaks when he could go up to level 10 if he wanted to when outside. For carpet time, a level 1 was negotiated, when David pointed out that it could never be totally silent as 'we all have to breathe!'.

After a couple of weeks the strategy had worked so well that only the Social Stories and timetable were needed Hodgson (2009).

Both these accounts by staff experienced in working with the difficult behaviours of pupils with Asperger syndrome highlight critical aspects of intervention:

- the amount of careful investigation needed to identify the purpose or function of the behaviour;
- the value of including the class and staff team, and implementing a holistic approach;
- the effectiveness of visual support that is inventively applied;
- the importance of reducing confusion and addressing social understanding;
- the need to motivate the pupil on his own terms;
- above all, the number of strategies which may be needed and the degree of flexibility and level of co-operation required between staff.

Summary

When behaviour difficulties occur, intervene systematically, basing interventions on careful, informed, methodical observation and data collection:

- Make a plan of action.
- Identify positive behaviours, strengths and skills.
- Specify the purpose or function of the behaviour for the child.
- Define the nature of the difficult behaviours precisely.
- Complete careful observations and record setting conditions, triggers for behaviours, ensuing actions or events and the results or outcomes.
- Design the intervention programme, concentrating efforts on introducing, reinforcing and extending appropriate and desired behaviours, to bring about long-term improvements.
- Use graded change techniques.
- Relate rewards to the child. Ensure they are meaningful, powerful, consistent and predictable.
- Consider using obsessive interests as reinforcers or rewards, as a way of introducing more acceptable behaviours and to increase desired skills.
- Monitor results – that is, keep recording!
- Evaluate outcomes against the original aims and redesign the programme if necessary.

Towards precision in assessment and teaching

Starting points

Once it has been established that Asperger syndrome is at the root of the child's difficulties, it is possible to extend our understanding of him. Initially, it is all too easy to see only the difficulties, and to be overwhelmed by them. It is necessary to establish a starting point for understanding and intervention. As one teacher said, 'I don't need any special equipment, I just need to understand Bethany in order to help her.' Hans Asperger described these children as 'troublesome but fascinating'.

Observation leading to intervention

It is easy to lose sight of the child within the syndrome, particularly if he is a member of a large class. It is only by observing children and reflecting on these observations that we begin to see and understand any situation. We make assumptions about children all the time. Careful observation, over a period of time, enables us to test these assumptions against the reality of the situation.

Following observations, a baseline can be established. Then it is possible to plan the way forward, putting into practice interventions designed to extend the experiences of the child and so facilitate his learning.

Use this profile format to help identify the child's particular areas of need within Asperger syndrome.

Part 1: word picture

One head teacher summarised a ten-year-old boy in a mainstream class of 32 children under the following headings:

- 'a very strange, bizarre, little chap';
- 'he's unpredictable';
- 'it's difficult to know when he's happy';
- 'it's quite easy to see *when* he's distressed, but difficult to know *why* he's distressed';
- 'he's slightly isolated'.

This general summary gives a brief 'word picture' of the child. It is necessary to zoom in from the wide focus in order to find starting points for the planning of intervention. Children with Asperger syndrome share the same core difficulties, but each child displays these difficulties in an individual way.

Part 2: observed behaviours

Part 2 of the profile itemises behaviours characteristic of Asperger syndrome. Not every child will display all the behaviours to the same extent. The profile gives the observer the opportunity to judge the extent to which the child's behaviours cause concern. For example:

Part 2	Observed behaviours				
1. Social interaction	1	2	3	4	5
a) ability to use gesture, body posture, facial expression and eye-to-eye gaze in 1:1 situations			✓		
b) ability to use gesture, body posture, facial expression and eye-to-eye gaze in group interaction					✓
c) ability to follow social cues in 1:1 with adults					✓
d) ability to follow social cues in 1:1 with other children				✓	

Level of concern: 1 – No cause for concern
2 – Mild cause for concern
3 – Moderate cause for concern
4 – Serious cause for concern
5 – Great cause for concern

In this example, the child's ability to use non-verbal communication in a group situation is causing great concern, although it is of less concern in one-to-one settings. His ability to follow social cues is also a major concern.

On completion of the profile, consideration should be given to the settings in which the child presents the greatest concern. It is then often possible to recognise a pattern, which, in turn, guides intervention.

Part 3: interpretation

At this point it will be useful to apply the Asperger lens to the concerns which have been prioritised. Use your understanding of Asperger syndrome to help identify the source of the child's difficulties. For example:

Part 3	Concerns	Possible sources
	The child rarely gives eye-to-eye contact in 1:1 settings.	Difficulty in understanding non-verbal communication.
	He can't talk and look at the same time.	Poor social skills.

Part 4: intervention planning

At this stage, it is useful to bring together parents and professionals in order to compare views. This meeting should result in the production of an agreed intervention plan. For example:

Part 4	**Intervention plan**
Targets	Strategies
Child to be able to relate a sequence of three events.	1. Take photos of the child involved in the event.
	2. Group the photos into sequences of three.
	3. Get the child to reflect on what he did, then to put the photos in the correct order.
	4. Let him use the photos as prompts as he relates what happened.

Evaluation

Set a period of time for the initial intervention. At the end of this period, use the schedule again to assess how the child's profile has changed and the amount of progress which has been made.

Note: The profile is not intended to be a diagnostic checklist although it may support the collection of evidence within a diagnostic process. It is designed to give teachers information about a child's strengths and weaknesses within Asperger syndrome and to provide starting points for intervention.

Observation profile

Part 1: Give a brief 'word picture' of the child within the class, noting positive points as well as difficulties.

Part 2: Observed behaviours

Key: 1 No cause for concern

2 Mild cause for concern

3 Moderate cause for concern

4 Serious cause for concern

5 Great cause for concern

1. Social interaction	1	2	3	4	5
a) ability to use gesture, body posture, facial expression and eye-to-eye gaze in 1:1 situation					
b) ability to use gesture, body posture, facial expression and eye-to-eye gaze in group interaction					
c) ability to follow social cues in 1:1 with adults					
d) ability to follow social cues in 1:1 with other children					
e) ability to follow social cues in group interaction					
f) ability to share an activity with other children					
g) ability to share an activity with an adult					
h) ability to develop peer friendships					
i) ability to seek comfort/affection when upset					
j) ability to offer comfort/affection to others					
k) ability to share in others' enjoyment/pleasure					
l) ability to imitate other children					

m) ability to imitate adults					
n) ability to show different responses to different people in different situations					
o) ability to respond appropriately to social praise					
p) ability to respond appropriately to criticism					

Comments

2. Social communication	1	2	3	4	5
a) ability to respond when called by name					
b) ability to follow verbal instructions in 1:1 setting					
c) ability to follow verbal instructions in a small group setting					
d) ability to follow verbal instructions in a whole class setting					
e) ability to take turns in conversations					
f) ability to initiate conversation					
g) ability to change topic of conversation					
h) ability to maintain an appropriate conversation					
i) ability to show awareness of the listener's needs					
j) ability to give appropriate non-verbal signals as a listener					
k) ability to change the topic or style of a conversation to suit the listener					
l) ability to appropriately change the volume and tone of voice					
m) ability to recognise and respond to non-verbal cues e.g. a frown)					
n) ability to understand implied meanings					

	1	2	3	4	5
o) ability to tell or write an imaginative story					
p) ability to relate a sequence of events					
q) ability to give a simple sequence of instructions					

Comments

3. Social imagination and flexible thinking	1	2	3	4	5
a) ability to have varied interests					
b) ability to share interests					
c) ability to change behaviour according to the situation					
d) ability to accept changes in rules, routines or procedures					
e) ability to play imaginatively when alone					
f) ability to play imaginatively together with others					
g) ability to accept others' points of view					
h) ability to generalise learning					
i) ability to transfer skills across the curriculum					
j) ability to plan an event or a task					
k) ability to suggest possible explanations for events					
l) ability to use inference and deduction					

Comments

4. Motor and organisational skills	1	2	3	4	5
a) ability to find his way around the classroom					
b) ability to find his way around the school					
c) ability to sit still					
d) ability to sit amongst a small group					
e) ability to sit amongst a large group (e.g. in assembly)					
f) ability to find and organise the equipment he needs for a given task					
g) ability to write legibly and draw accurately					
h) ability to get changed without help (e.g. for PE)					
i) ability to organise his movements in PE and games					

Comments

5. Learning style: evidences	1	2	3	4	5
a) superior ability in restricted area of interest, while having average to above average skills in other areas					
b) an extreme or obsessive interest in a narrow subject					
c) focused and prolonged concentration on topics of interest to self *(with limited attention to other tasks or topics)*					
d) skills in reading (i.e. decoding) which exceed comprehension					
e) computational skills in numeracy which exceed problem-solving skills					
f) an unusually excellent rote memory					
g) better functioning when engaged in familiar or routine tasks					

	1	2	3	4	5
h) better functioning when tasks are presented visually					
i) a striking lack of common sense					
j) overall average or above average level of ability compared to same age peers					

Comments

6. Sensory issues: evidences	1	2	3	4	5
a) unusual reactions to loud, unpredictable sounds (e.g. may try to block out sounds)					
b) overreaction to strong or artificial light					
c) overreacts to certain smells that are hardly recognizable to others					
d) intolerant of the feel of certain fabrics					
e) hyposensitivity to discomfort or pain					
f) rejection of common flavours or textures in food					
g) sensation-seeking in movement (e.g. rocking, spinning or swinging)					
h) frequently stiffens, flinches or pulls away when hugged					

Comments

Note the settings in which the child shows anxiety, stress or frustration (e.g. during PE, in the Hall, at transition times, when sitting amongst a large group).

Prioritise the three difficulties which cause you the greatest concern.

1	
2	
3	

Part 3: Concerns	Possible sources

Part 4: intervention plan

Targets	Strategies

Appendix
Diagnostic criteria for Asperger syndrome

From *ICD 10* (World Health Organisation 1992)

A. A lack of any clinically significant delay in language or cognitive development.

Diagnosis requires that single words should have developed by two years of age or earlier and that communicative phrases be used by three years of age or earlier. Self-help skills, adaptive behaviour and curiosity about the environment during the first three years should be at a level consistent with normal intellectual development. However, motor milestones may be somewhat delayed and motor clumsiness is usual (although not a necessary diagnostic feature). Isolated special skills, often related to abnormal preoccupations, are common, but are not required for diagnosis.

B. Qualitative impairments in reciprocal social interaction (criteria as for autism).

Diagnosis requires demonstrable abnormalities in at least 3 out of the following 5 areas:

1. failure adequately to use eye-to-eye gaze, facial expression, body posture and gesture to regulate social interaction;
2. failure to develop (in a manner appropriate to mental age, and despite ample opportunities) peer relationships that involve a mutual sharing of interests, activities and emotions;
3. rarely seeking and using other people for comfort and affection at times of stress or distress and/or offering comfort and affection to others when they are showing distress or unhappiness;
4. lack of shared enjoyment in terms of vicarious pleasure in other people's happiness and/or a spontaneous seeking to share their own enjoyment through joint involvement with others;
5. a lack of socio-emotional reciprocity as shown by an impaired or deviant response to other people's emotions; and/or lack of modulation of behaviour according to social context, and/or a weak integration of social, emotional and communicative behaviours.

C. Restricted, repetitive and stereotyped patterns of behaviour, interests and activities.

(Criteria as for autism; however it would be less usual for these to include either motor mannerisms or preoccupations with part-objects or non-functional elements of play materials).

Diagnosis requires demonstrable abnormalities in at least 2 out of the following 6 areas:

1. an encompassing preoccupation with stereotyped and restricted patterns of interest;
2. specific attachments to unusual objects;
3. apparently compulsive adherence to specific, non-functional, routines or rituals;
4. stereotyped and repetitive motor mannerisms that involve either hand/finger flapping or twisting, or complex whole body movement;
5. preoccupations with part-objects or non-functional elements of play materials (such as their odour, the feel of their surface, or the noise/vibration that they generate);
6. distress over changes in small, non-functional, details of the environment.

D. The disorder is not attributable to the other varieties of pervasive developmental disorder; schizotypal disorder; simple schizophrenia; reactive and disinhibited attachment disorder of childhood; obsessional personality disorder; obsessive compulsive disorder.

From *DSM IV* (American Psychiatric Association 1994)

A. Qualitative impairment in social interaction as manifested by at least two of the following:

1. marked impairment in the use of multiple non-verbal behaviours such as eye-to-eye gaze, facial expression, body postures and gestures to regulate social interaction.
2. failure to develop peer relationships appropriate to developmental level.
3. a lack of spontaneous seeking to share enjoyment, interests or achievements with other people (eg: by a lack of showing, bringing, or pointing out objects of interest to other people).
4. lack of social or emotional reciprocity.

B. Restricted, repetitive and stereotyped patterns of behaviour, interests and activities, as manifested by at least one of the following:

1. encompassing preoccupation with one or more stereotyped and restricted patterns of interest that is abnormal either in intensity or focus.
2. apparently inflexible adherence to specific, non-functional routines or rituals.
3. stereotyped and repetitive motor mannerisms (eg: hand or finger flapping or twisting, or complex whole body movements).
4. persistent preoccupation with parts of objects.

C. The disturbance causes clinically significant impairment in social, occupational or other important areas of functioning.

D. There is no clinically significant general delay in language (eg: single words used by 2 years, communicative phrases used by age 3 years).

E. There is no clinically significant delay in cognitive development or in the development of age-appropriate self-help skills, adaptive behaviour (other than in social interaction), and curiosity about the environment in childhood.

F. Criteria are not met for another specific Pervasive Developmental Disorder or Schizophrenia.

References

American Psychiatric Association (1987) *Diagnostic and Statistical Manual of Mental Disorders*, 3rd edition – revised (*DSM III-R*). Washington: American Psychiatric Association.

American Psychiatric Association (1994) *Diagnostic and Statistical Manual of Mental Disorders*, 4th edition (*DSM IV*). Washington: American Psychiatric Association.

Asperger, H. (1944) 'Die "autistischen Psychopathen" im Kindesalter', *Archiv fur Psychiatrie und Nervenkrankheiten* 117: 76–136. English translation in Frith, U. (ed.) (1991).

Autism Centre for Education and Research (ACER) (2009) *Educational Provision for Children and Young People on the Autism Spectrum Living in England: A Review of Current Practice, Issues and Challenges*. London: Autism Education Trust.

Autism Working Group (2002) *Autistic Spectrum Disorders: Good Practice Guidance*. London: DfES.

Baird, G., Simonoff, E., Pickles, A., Chandler, S., Loucas, T., Meldrum, D. *et al.* (2006) 'Prevalence of disorders of the autistic spectrum in a populationcohort of children in South Thames: the Special Needs and Autism Project (SNAP)', *Lancet* 368 (9531): 210–15.

Baron-Cohen, S. (1990) 'Autism: a specific cognitive disorder of "Mind Blindness"', *International Journal of Psychiatry* 2: 81–90.

Baron-Cohen, S. (1996) *Mindblindness. An Essay on Autism and Theory of Mind*. Cambridge, MA: MIT Press.

Baron-Cohen, S., Leslie, A.M. and Frith, U. (1985) 'Does the autistic child have a Theory of Mind?', *Cognition* 21: 37–46.

Bellini, S. (2004) 'Social skills deficits and anxiety in high functioning adolescents with autism spectrum disorders', *Focus on Autism and Other Developmental Disabilities* 19(2): 78–86.

Bishop, D. (2003) *Children's Communication Checklist (CCC-2)*. London: Psychological Corporation.

Bleuler, E. (1911) *Dementia praecox oder gruppe der schizophrenien* (J. Zinkin translation 1950). New York: International University Press.

Buron, K.D. and Curtis, M. (2003) *The Incredible 5-Point Scale – Assisting Children with Autistic Spectrum Disorders in Understanding Social Interactions and in Controlling their Emotional Responses*. Shawnee Mission, KS: Autism Asperger Publishing Co.

DfES (2003) *Every Child Matters – Change for Children*. London: DfES Publications.

Ehlers, S. and Gillberg, C. (1993) 'The epidemiology of Asperger syndrome: a total population study', *Journal of Child Psychology and Psychiatry* 34: 1327–50.

Evans, G. (1997) 'The development of the outdoor education programme at Storm House School', in S. Powell and R. Jordan, *Autism and Learning*. London: David Fulton.

Fitzpatrick, E. (2004) 'The use of cognitive behavioural strategies in the management of anger in a child with autistic spectrum disorder', *Good Autism Practice* 5(1): 3–17.

Frith, U. (1989) *Autism, Explaining the Enigma*. Oxford: Basil Blackwell.

Frith, U. (ed.) (1991) *Autism and Asperger Syndrome*. Cambridge: Cambridge University Press.

Ghaziuddin, M. (2005) *Mental Health Aspects of Autism and Asperger Syndrome*. London: Jessica Kingsley.

Gillberg, C. (1989) 'Asperger syndrome in 23 Swedish children', *Developmental Medicine and Child Neurology* 31: 520–31.

Gillberg, C. (1990) 'Autism and pervasive developmental disorders', *Journal of Child Psychology and Psychiatry* 31: 99–119.

Gillberg, C. (1991) 'Clinical and neurobiological aspects of Asperger syndrome in 6 family studies', in U. Frith (ed.), *Autism and Asperger Syndrome*. Cambridge: Cambridge University Press.

Gillberg, C. and Coleman, M. (1992) *The Biology of the Autistic Syndromes*. London: MacKeith.

Gilliam, J.E. (2003) *Gilliam Autism Rating Scale (GARS)*. Austin, TX: Pro-ed.

Goldman-Rakic, P. (1987) 'Development of cortical circuitry and cognitive function', *Child Development* 58: 601–22.

Grandin, T. and Scariano, M. (1986) *Emergence, Labelled Autistic*. Tunbridge Wells: Costello.

Gray, C. (1994a) *Comic Strip Conversations*. Arlington, TX: Future Horizons.

Gray, C. (1994b) *The Original Social Story Book*. Arlington, TX: Future Horizons.

Gray, C. (2002) *My Social Stories Book*. London: Jessica Kingsley.

Gray, C. and Howley, M. (2005) *Revealing the Hidden Social Code*. London: Jessica Kingsley.

Green, J. (1990) 'Is Asperger's a syndrome?' *Developmental Medicine and Child Neurology* 32: 743–7.

Greig, A. and McKay, T. (2005) *Asperger's Syndrome and Cognitive Behaviour Therapy: New Applications for Educational Psychologists*. London: Educational and Child Psychology.

Happé, F. (1994) *Autism, an Introduction to Psychological Theory*. London: UCL Press.

Happé, F. and Frith, U. (1995) 'Theory of mind in autism', in E. Schopler and G.B. Mesibov (eds), *Learning and Cognition in Autism*. New York: Plenum Press.

Hare, D. (1997) 'The use of cognitive behaviour therapy with people with Asperger syndrome', *Autism* 1: 215–25.

Hare, D.J. (2004) 'Developing cognitive behavioural work with people with ASD', *Good Autism Practice* 5: 18–22.

Hare, D.J. and Paine, C. (1997) *Developing Cognitive Behavioural Treatments for People with Asperger's Syndrome*, Clinical Psychology Forum, December.

Harries, D. (2008) Personal communication.

Hobson, P. (1993) *Autism and the Development of Mind*. Hove: Laurence Erlbaum.

Hodgson, H. (2009) Personal communication.

Howell, L. (2004) *Exam Advice for Young People with Autism and Asperger Syndrome*. London: National Autistic Society.

Howlin, P. and Rutter, M. (1987) *Treatment of Autistic Children*. Chichester: John Wiley.

Jarman, J. (2008) *Hangman*. London: Collins.

Jordan, R. and Powell, S. (1995) *Understanding and Teaching Children with Autism*. Chichester: Wiley.

Kanner, L. (1943) 'Autistic disturbance of affective contact', *Nervous Child* 2: 217–50.

Kim, J.A., Szatmari, P., Bryson, S.E., Streiner, D.L. and Wilson, F.J. (2000) 'The prevalence of anxiety and mood problems among children with autism and Asperger syndrome', *Autism: the International Journal of Research & Practice* 4(2): 117–32.

Le Couteur, A., Rutter, M., Lord, C., Rios, P., Robertson, S., Holdgrafer, M. and McLennan, J. (1989) 'Autism diagnostic interview: a standardised investigator-based instrument', *Journal of Autism and Developmental Disorders* 19: 363–89.

Lord, C. (1995) 'Treatment of a high-functioning adolescent with autism: a cognitive-behavioral approach', in M.A. Reinecke and F.M. Dattilio (eds), *Cognitive Therapy with Children and Adolescents: A Casebook for Clinical Practice*, 394–404. New York: Guilford.

Lord, C., Rutter, M., Goode, S., Heemsbergen, J., Jordan, H., Mawhood, L. and Schopler, E. (1989) 'Autism diagnostic observation schedule: a standardised observation of communicative and social behaviour', *Journal of Autism and Developmental Disorders* 19: 185–97.

Lord, C. Rutter, M., DiLavore, P.C. and Risi, S. (1999) *Autism Diagnostic Observation Schedule*. Los Angeles: Western Psychological Services.

Luria, A.R. (1966) *The Higher Cortical Functions in Man*. New York: Basic Books.

Madsen, C.H., Becker, W.C. and Thomas, D.R. (1968) 'Rules, praise and ignoring: elements of elementary classroom control', *Journal of Applied Behavioural Analysis* 1: 139–50.

Mesibov, G. (2009) *Evidence-based Practice in Autism Lecture to Meeting of Minds Conference*. Herning: Denmark.

Mesibov, G. and Faherty, C. (2000) *Asperger's – What Does it Mean to Me*. Arlington, TX: Future Horizons.

Mesibov, G. and Howley, M. (2003) *Accessing the Curriculum for Pupils with Autistic Spectrum Disorders – using the TEACCH programme to help inclusion*. London: David Fulton.

Moran. H.J. (2005) 'Working with angry children', in P. Cummins (ed.), *Working with Anger*. Chichester: Wiley.

National Initiative for Autism Screening and Assessment (NIASA) (2003) *National Autism Plan*. London: National Autistic Society.

National Strategies (2009) *Supporting Children on the Autism Spectrum*. London: DfES.

National Strategies (2009) *Supporting Pupils on the Autism Spectrum*. London: DfES.

Newton, C. and Wilson, D. (1999) *Circles of Friends*. London: Folens.

Newson, E. (1992) Enabling flexibility and social empathy in able autistic children: some practical strategies. Unpublished paper. Arhus Conference, October 1992.

References

Ozonoff, S. (1995) 'Executive functions in autism', in E, Schopler and G.B. Mesibov (eds), *Learning and Cognition in Autism*. New York: Plenum Press.

Peers, J. (1997) An Asperger's guide to obsessions. Unpublished booklet.

Perner, J., Frith, U., Leslie, A.M. and Leekham, S.R. (1989) 'Exploration of the autistic child's Theory of Mind: knowledge, belief and communication', *Child Development* 60: 689–700.

Powell, S.D. and Jordan, R. (eds) (1997) *Autism and Learning: A Guide to Good Practice*. London: David Fulton.

Reaven, J. and Hepburn, S. (2003) 'Cognitive behavioural treatment of obsessive compulsive disorder in a child with Asperger syndrome', *Autism* 7(2): 145–64.

Rinaldi, W. (1992) *The Social Use of Language Programme*. Windsor: NFER–Nelson.

Roid, G.H. and Miller, L.J. (1997) *Leiter International Performance Scale – Revised*. Los Angeles: Western Psychological Services.

Rutter, M. (1978) 'Language disorder and infantile autism', in M. Rutter and E. Schopler (eds), *Autism: A Reappraisal of Concepts and Treatments*. New York: Plenum Press.

Schopler, E., Mesibov, G.B. and Hearsey, K. (1995) 'Structured teaching in the TEACCH system', in E. Schopler and G.B. Mesibov (eds), *Learning and Cognition in Autism*. New York: Plenum Press.

Schopler, E., Reichler, R.J., Bashford, A., Lansing, M.D. and Marcus, L.M. (1990) *Psychoeducational Profile – Revised (PEP-R)*. Austin, TX: Pro-Ed.

Schopler, E., Reichler, R.J., DeVellis, R.F. and Daily, K. (1980) 'Towards objective classification of childhood autism: Childhood Autism Rating Scale', *Journal of Austism and Developmental Disorders* 10: 91–101.

Tantam, D. (1987) *A Mind of One's Own*. London: National Autistic Society.

Tantam, D. (1988) 'Lifelong eccentricity and social isolation: Asperger syndrome or Schizoid Personality Disorder?' *British Journal of Psychiatry* 153: 783–91.

Tantam, D. (1997) Unpublished paper.

Vermeulen, P. (2001) *Autistic Thinking*. London: Jessica Kingsley.

Warnock Report (1978) *Special Educational Needs*. London: HMSO.

Wechsler, D. (1991) *Wechsler Intelligence Scale for Children (WISC)*. New York: Harcourt Brace Jovanovich.

Whitaker, P., Barrett, P., Joy, H. and Thomas, G. (1998) 'Children with autism and peer group support: using Circles of Friends', *British Journal of Special Education* 25(2): 60–4.

Williams, D. (1996) *Autism: An Inside Out Approach*. London: Jessica Kingsley.

Winner, M.G. (2002) *Thinking About You, Thinking About Me*. San Jose, CA: Think Social Publishing Inc.

Wing, L. (1981a) 'Language, social and cognitive impairments in autism and severe mental retardation', *Journal of Autism and Developmental Disorders* 11: 31–44.

Wing, L. (1981b) 'Asperger's syndrome: a clinical account', *Journal of Psychological Medicine* 11: 115–29.

Wing, L. (1991) 'The relationship between Asperger's syndrome and Kanner's autism', in U. Frith (ed.), *Autism and Asperger Syndrome*. Cambridge: Cambridge University Press.

Wing, L. (1996) *The Autistic Spectrum*. London: Constable.

Wing, L. and Gould, J. (1979) 'Severe impairments of social interaction and associated abnormalities in children: epidemiology and classification', *Journal of Autism and Childhood Schizophrenia* 9: 11–29.

Witkin, H.A., Oltman, P.K., Roskin, E. and Karp, S. (1971) *A Manual for the Embedded Figures Test*. Palo Alto, CA: Consulting Psychologists Press.

Wolff, S. (1995) *Loners: The Life Path of Unusual Children*. London: Routledge.

World Health Organisation (1978) *International Statistical Classification of Diseases and Related Health Problems*, 9th edition (*ICD 9*). Geneva: World Health Organisation.

World Health Organisation (1992) *International Statistical Classification of Diseases and Related Health Problems*, 10th edition (*ICD 10*). Geneva: World Health Organisation.

Zarkowska, E. and Clements, J. (1988) *Problem Behaviour in People with Severe Learning Difficulties*. London: Croom Helm.

Index

ADHD (Attention Deficit Hyperactivity Disorder) 13
ADI (Autism Diagnostic Interview) 16–17
ADOS (Autism Diagnostic Observation Schedule) 16, 17
aggressiveness 81
anxiety 46, 53, 83, 84; about examinations 60; reducing 55, 85
anxiety disorders 80–2
Armitage, David 54
Asperger, Hans 1, 12, 43
Asperger learning style 57–8; strategies for examinations 60–2
Asperger syndrome 1–2; key features 5–7
assemblies, coping with 63
assessment 11–12; approaches to 14–16; contribution of teachers 19–21; multidisciplinary 13–14; tools for 16–19
attention 29, 58
Attention Deficit Hyperactivity Disorder (ADHD) 13
autism 1–2, 22; diagnostic criteria 3, 12; triad of impairments 2–3, 22
Autism Centre for Education and Research 38
Autism Diagnostic Interview 16–17
Autism Diagnostic Observation Schedule 16, 17
Autism Education Trust 42
autism spectrum pathways 16

Bannister, Lynda 78, 79
Baron-Cohen, Simon 23, 69
behaviour 25, 63; help with 46, 47; inappropriate 5, 6, 84; obsessive 46, 47, 71; predicting and understanding others' 25, 26, 69, 70; rigidity of 31, 46, 71, 81; stress and 78–80
behaviour management 72–7, 78–80; case studies 73–8, 91–3; school environment and 84–7; specific interventions 87–91
Bishop, Dorothy 17
Bleuler, E. 1
Block Design Test 29
boys, and Asperger syndrome 1, 3, 4
brain 4, 31
'Bubble Dialogue' (computer program) 91
buddy system 53–4, 63
bullying 1, 39, 53, 77, 82; reducing 82–3
Buron, K.D. 90

CAMHS (Child and Adolescent Mental Health Services) 81, 82
care plans 15

CARS (Childhood Autism Rating Scale) 17
case studies 7–11, 41, 67, 68, 73–8, 81, 91–3
Central Coherence Deficit 28–9; implications of 29–31
change: gradual 89; preparing for 85; resistance to 2, 3, 6, 29
Child and Adolescent Mental Health Services (CAMHS) 81, 82
Childhood Autism Rating Scale 17
Children's Communication Checklist 17–18
Children's Embedded Figures Test 28, 29
children's literature, children with autism in 54
Children's Plan 37
Children's Trusts 34
choice, difficulty in making 30, 31, 59
circle of friends 54, 64
class teachers 19, 57, 63, 65–6; assessment by 19–21; role of 44, 45, 46
classrooms 44,76; organisation and structure 48–51; seating arrangements 65, 66
clumsiness 7, 13, 46
cognitive ability, assessment of 18
cognitive behaviour therapy 90
Collis, Len 52
comic strip conversations 90–1
communication (*see also* social communication) 17, 51; language environment 51–2; with Asperger children 46–7
comprehension difficulties 61, 62; modified examination papers to allow for 62
compulsivity 71
computers, use of 61, 72
confidence 45
conscience, lack of 26
context, making sense of events in 29
conversation 20, 26, 51; initiating 64; teaching skills 65
creative writing 58
curriculum (*see also* National Curriculum): flexibility of 37, 38

debriefing sessions 90–1
decoding 58, 69
depression 81
detail, preference for 29, 31
diagnosis 11–12, 103–4; criteria 3, 12; differential 12–13; teachers' contribution to 19–21
Diagnostic and Statistical Manual 3, 12, 14, 104–5
Diagnostic Interview for Social and Communication Disorders (DISCO) 15, 16
dining rooms 64–5
diplomas 38